Women of Honor

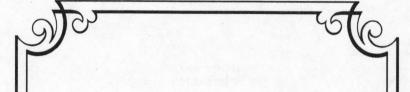

Women of Honor

God's Incredible Plan for Fulfillment

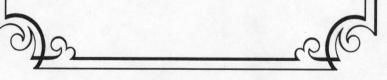

Jeanne Hendricks

Part One

THE DIVINE PERSPECTIVE OF WOMEN

Part Two

HOW DOES SHE FUNCTION?

Part Three

WHY IS SHE
IMPORTANT?

Part Four

HOW CAN GOD'S WOMANHOOD FIT ME?

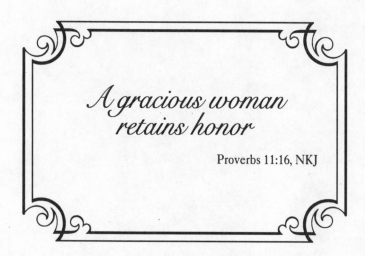

A gracious woman retains honor

Proverbs 11:16, NKJ

In the Beginning

❧

$\mathscr{E}$ver since the first woman flirted with the fiction that God was somehow unfair when He labeled certain fruit off-limits, females have been floundering. A casual glance at any history book, ancient or modern, hints at a kind of black hole into which most women have disappeared. Art, literature and military exploits largely comprise our tracings of yesteryear, but very few credit lines are assigned to women. You and I who have been to school are asking why.

In our century the feminist freight train has roared into courtrooms and legislative assemblies. Women are waving gavels and rewriting text books in a frenzy of reform unequaled in history. Masculine defendants in sexual discrimination lawsuits are numb with shock. If published reports are believed, we seem to have reached a suspenseful scene in the western world drama where the irate protagonist has consigned her children to some custodian and now stands smirking astride her hand-cuffed male partner, daring him to whisper that she is the weaker sex.

Most of the years during this erratic century have been imprinted on my personal memory. Before I could read, I absorbed the intense energy of my parents as they inhaled the euphoria of the "Roaring Twenties." I watched wide-eyed as the dust of the Great Depression settled over our big city. To impress on my wondering mind that our money was gone and we had to move, my father drove past the iron-barred doors of our bank. Slowly the engines of war jump-started our gray world and I embraced adulthood trying to sort out conflicting messages of fear and faith. I puzzled over how to play my role as a woman: Was it a principal character or just a bit part?

Always there has been a persistent question: Why am I a girl? Early on I met God personally and found Him to be good, compassionate and completely trustworthy. He obviously controls all of life, so for sovereign reasons He allows Hindenberg disasters and Hitler-like lunacy—as well as the tiny technicality that made me female.

My older sister was born to family fanfare in granddad's farmhouse, welcomed by adoring aunts and cousins at a proper time of year. The crops were harvested and everybody rejoiced over the new baby.

When I showed up on a cold January afternoon in the bedroom of a rented city townhouse, only Dad was there to heat the water and show the hired nurse up the stairs. The family simply said they had "another girl"—nothing too exciting. But somehow I came to know my presence here was no ho-hum affair with an all-wise God. Then

He graciously dropped a theologian into my life as a marriage partner, and I knew intuitively that I would find out what my Maker had in mind.

If women, by and large, are blanked out of history; if baby girls are considered expendable; if statistics consistently show females to be abused and exploited, I wanted to know why. Being a born teacher, my husband wouldn't think of giving me answers to my endless questions. He simply pointed to the Bible and assured me that in its inspired pages the Holy Spirit had included the solution to every little doubt I might devise.

I found the Bible to be dramatic and suspenseful reading, but at first it raised more questions than it answered. When God created the first woman, He pulled the curtain. All we know is that He took a surgically-removed portion of Adam's side and sculpted a breathtaking creature whom Adam adored. She was the crowning jewel of His creation.

When Satan, God's arch-enemy, locked on to the woman with evil intent, he honed his rhetoric to derail her. She discussed with him the unthinkable; disbelief of the Creator's word. After years of re-reading it, I finally saw three reasons: she saw that the fruit was good for food; it was pleasing to her senses; and it was desirable to make one wise. That's the way God made her. No sin was present until she yielded to the temptation. Now my fog was lifting.

After she disobeyed, the woman would face her Maker and plead not-guilty. It was, she said, the fault of the loudmouth serpent. God's eternal purposes, however, would not be thwarted; His holiness and justice would not be compromised. She would continue as Adam's wife; she would be the mother of all future generations. But she would—she must—face her responsibility for flouting Authority.

For every one of us who is born female, this is our personal history. We are Eve's daughters. She was deceived; are we twisting in the winds of deceit? We live with the painful consequences of disobedience. What to do?

Like digging out nuggets of precious stones, the simple study of what God has written forces me to declare that it all makes sense. Even though I cannot comprehend the magnitude of God's plan, I have found where I fit; I've got the hang of why females swim against the current. Best of all, I am assured that God has provided the upper hand for His erring daughters. Nothing has ever excited my passion to communicate God's Word so much as the electrifying truth that there is a divine solution to my personal struggle for significance.

No one ever finds truth alone. My debts are many. With Howie, my lover, my leader, my sometimes-exasperating in-house teacher and mentor for almost a half century, I am hopelessly awash in red ink. Too-many-to-count writers and speakers have diffused ideas and insights over the years, for which I am deeply thankful.

This book, however, would not be reality unless John Van Diest of Vision House Publishing had waved the green flag for me. But it is to my editor, Brenda Josee, most of all, that I must bow for her thoughtful expertise in crafting this volume, in corralling my stray sentences and bedding them down. May men and women who read these pages never again see Eve—or themselves—as anything less than the object of God's redeeming love.

Jeanne W. Hendricks

Our literary tour of womanhood will take us through realities and possibilities. From unchanging facts and promises we will extract foundational principles that will enable us to live with confidence. The first three chapters of Genesis provide a seed pod of six distinctively feminine hallmarks each validated by biblical portraits.

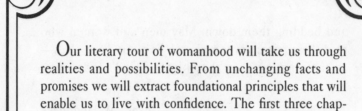

The Jewel

The Manager

The Beautician

The Investigator

The Caregiver

The Controller

These six distinctives are very precious to God. Just as they are threaded through His Word, so they are threaded through this book as we take our tour of womanhood.

To the present day they offer both dangerous pitfalls and limitless prospects. I, as a woman, can either stumble and fall or soar ahead. The outcome hinges on how well I grasp the life of faith which God offers. I need not war against the very distinctives God created but trust His promise to change my potential pitfalls into bright prospects. What He said is trustworthy; I can find it true...you too, can find it true.

Part One

THE DIVINE PERSPECTIVE OF WOMEN

THE JEWEL
Eve was created and positioned by God as His piece d'resistance of all that He had made. She was, therefore, the prime target for the tempter.

THE MANAGER
Woman wants what works. She naturally organizes her life to yield a profit.

THE BEAUTICIAN
Woman is built for beauty. She is naturally beautiful and she is stirred deeply when true loveliness touches her.

THE INVESTIGATOR
The urge to know more is a primary drive within a woman and because of it she is vulnerable to deception.

THE CAREGIVER
A woman's need to nurture energizes her relationships with a caring spirit in spite of obstacles.

THE CONTROLLER
Woman strives to take charge, concentrating her many capabilities on leadership goals, but apart from God's enablement she is frustrated.

Through Female Eyes

❧

She clutched her leather briefcase with ease and stepped back in the elevator as it emptied at the lobby. Eyeing her coworkers with the controlled confidence of a professional, she pressed a button and continued down to reserved parking, car keys in hand. Sliding behind the wheel of her sports car, she edged into the downtown traffic with a relaxed sigh. At a red light the car phone rang.

"Estelle, dear, I'm so glad I caught you. They told me you'd left the office and I am wondering if you would stop by to get Stephanie on the way home. I know it's my turn but I am really tied up here..."

"Doug!" she snapped at her husband, "You did the same thing only last week. This isn't fair!"

"I know, honey, but I can't help it. Our European rep just now arrived, got delayed in New York, and you know he's my responsibility. Maybe I could bring him home for dinner, huh? He really wants to meet you. Or, you could meet us...why don't you call me when you get home?"

By now Estelle was creeping along in heavy homebound lines of tail-lighted cars. She glanced at the dashboard clock.

"Doug, it's already nearly six o'clock. There's no way I can stop at the school, and have a guest for dinner. Oh well, I'll try to work out something and call you. Bye."

Traffic speeded up and Estelle's thoughts raced. *What have I gotten into? After three years I thought this marriage would smooth out. Poor little kid! Her own mother didn't want her and sometimes I wonder about Doug, even forgetting her birthday last month!. And now he wants me to get a babysitter tonight. For a seven-year-old that's not right.*

At the school, Stephanie obviously had been crying. The attendant explained that her father had called to say he could not come, and she was disappointed because she had made a special paper flower for him. Now she was afraid no one would come for her. Estelle tried to be loving and cheerful.

"Would you like to have a special dinner of your very own tonight? We could stop and buy something; what would you like?" Estelle asked.

"No, I just want Daddy. I'm not hungry."

Home at last, Estelle closed the garage door and gave Stephanie a warm hug, assuring her that she loved her very much, and that they both loved her Daddy and needed to understand when he could not be with them. As Stephanie trudged toward her room, was she sucking her thumb?

In the kitchen Estelle quickly rolled up her silk sleeves and started to thaw out chicken pieces for Stephanie's dinner. Meanwhile she eyed the note from the cleaning service about a plumbing problem and listened to messages on the answering machine: the repair shop with their radio, Doug's son at college. Then from the tape her mother's strained voice forced her to sit down and listen.

"Estelle, my dear, I hate to bother you. I don't know if it's serious or not, but your father is acting funny. He says he must see you, says he has to tell you something before he leaves. I don't know if it's kind of a premonition that he's going to die, or whether his mind is wandering. It's just not like him at all! He keeps saying he hopes Doug is treating you well and that he isn't sure he should have let you get married, especially to a man with children... I didn't mean to ramble...but I told him you're fine. After all you were 32...but anyhow, please try to call him tonight... and remember he goes to bed early. I'm sure he'll be all right if he hears your voice...well, I better go now."

Just as she started to call Stephanie, the phone rang.

"It's me again, honey. Why didn't you call me? Have you been trying to get a sitter? I have to do something about dinner..."

"The answer is no, Doug. I haven't got anybody to be with Stephanie and I've got to call my father... something's wrong...I'm sorry but you'd better go on without me...See you when you get home, honey."

How Come?

How does it all happen? How does a woman who tries to do things right find herself in a complicated maze, her dreams dissolving, her beliefs shattering? Why does she sometimes feel like the only attendant in a zoo full of hungry animals? Everyone in her life seems to want something from her. She fights to retain her own personhood.

How does another woman think for herself if she has been born into a home where no one ever asked her what she wanted? Another is grieving because she traded her self-respect for what looked like a good deal. Can she ever again feel self-esteem? Is there really hope for meaningful fulfillment?

Most of us in the Western world inherit beliefs about loving families that are based on the conviction that marriage is sacred, that women are to be honored, that children bless a home and that honest work is commendable. We have been taught that dignity demands an education and that we have a right to expect an orderly world that is peaceful and prosperous.

As the twenty-first century dawns on our horizon, however, many of us are trying to plug the dike against disaster. We find marriage has been downgraded to a temporary tryout; children are often gasping for a breath of sane understanding. Men are restless and confused. Education and civic pride sag to unsafe levels. Honest work ranks low on "to do" lists. Are we women stuck in a cul-de-sac, victims of some patriarchal conspiracy? Does God not like us?

A look at our lives might lead us to believe that

God never spoke on the subject of women. But He did! Not in a list of rules, but in selected reports of women who actually lived in diverse cultures under the most defiant circumstances; divine diaries that serve as a kind of control tower to guide women toward His love and safety. We have largely missed His message, His insistent whisper that woman is valuable, needed, the divine linchpin uniquely designed to nourish the human race.

Sometimes our sea is calm and we are lulled into romantic dreams, but more often, like Estelle's seemingly successful life, the waves are rolling. If we do not understand the source of the currents, the winds, the unyielding power of history which drives our world, we may easily run aground. Perhaps even more vital is to discern how we ourselves are programmed—not exploring the add-ons or improvements, but the basic design which identifies us as women.

What's It All About

How far back shall we go for a reliable chart? How can we pinpoint our location and project a disaster-free future? Whose word is valid, whose historical record accurate?

My search took me to the Bible because only God is sovereign. His prophets have spoken:

Do you not know? Have you not heard? Has it not been told you from the beginning? Have you not understood since the earth was founded? He sits enthroned...He stretches out the heavens...He brings

23

princes to naught...The Lord is the everlasting God, the Creator of the ends of the earth (Isaiah. 40:21-28).

I am the Lord your God who teaches you what is best for you, who directs you in the way you should go (Isaiah 48:17).

The biblical Scriptures light our paths, but we must understand that the Bible is not primarily about women. It is the record of God's plan to rescue all people from the impossible sin predicament. Pathos and suspense clothe the characters; the knowledge that the women described are real and the events are history makes it instructive. What God has to say about women becomes critically important in whatever case we construct for the female sex.

A kind of archeological dig is possible through the Sacred Scriptures from the dawn of history through to the early Christian era. Like pieces of perfectly preserved pottery, each woman described reveals a vein of rich information—cultural habits, personal quirks, and more importantly God's commands and critiques.

Marriage, motherhood, widowhood, working women and royalty are presented in the biblical records, complete with editorial comment. A close scrutiny of what He says is like finding answers in the back of life's exam book. Womanhood suddenly makes sense and becomes a priceless privilege.

Woman: God's Crowning Achievement

Somewhere between sophomore daze and senior semi-ignorance in my high school career, I began to see myself as a woman. Like the famous "little engine that could," I was beginning to build up a head of steam as I struggled up the hill toward adulthood.

The national mood was militaristic. In the wake of Pearl Harbor every man, woman and child was expected to pitch in and help fight the enemy. I hurried as fast as possible to tear off the togs of childhood and climb into adult robes. Finally, exhilarated with the grandeur of a diploma, I willingly postponed higher education and signed on with a large company to type lengthy requisitions for eight hours every day.

"This is the real world," my family and friends assured me. With high hopes I became a daily "strap-hanger" on a crowded trolley rattling toward city-center. At the office I became acquainted with the files and the people and the machines—all pretty much alike. I learned to live with the choking cigar smoke from my supervisor across the aisle. With good timing and speed, I could dodge the foreman who made passes at me when I went into the stockroom for supplies. The job settled into a routine of daily doings with few headline features. The world, I learned, had a deadening sameness about it that wore people down to autistic blobs.

At a Christmas dinner where attendance was mandatory, I discovered the office workers had a bawdy sublayer. With a little liquor the men unleashed an ugly machismo and the women became wanton coquettes. Fortunately I had to leave early.

Not too many months later the personnel manager narrowed his eyes and looked at my resignation form I had brought to his desk. "You're probably making a wise decision," he said flatly. "You really belong in college. Good luck."

I cleaned out my desk and took the elevator down to the noisy street for the last time. I had wanted so much to be a part, but I was on a different wavelength. Why? My questions were unformed, but they were beginning to develop inside my head.

Were the preachers really right, that a woman's place is in the home? Is a woman, after all, really meant to be the plaything of a man? Why this geyser inside; this irrepressible desire to learn about things and study people and answer riddles? Some of the solutions came years later when I visited the Garden of Eden via the Book of Genesis.

The Perfect Triangle: Adam-Eve-God

The Garden of Eden houses a well-packed para-chute out of which stream all of the history, science, "ologies" and "isms" known to man. Life in the garden is more than just an intriguing story of God's fashioning a woman to integrate the life of the first man. It is more than just a dramatic scenario from the ancient past. Thereon hangs—not a tale, but a trail—a path that leads right to your front door and mine.

With this single exception of Eden, beginnings have always been hard. For instance, I remember reading about the first two white women on the Oregon Trail.

In the 1830s a medical doctor and a Presbyterian minister, Marcus Whitman and Henry Spalding, set out for Fort Vancouver with their new brides, Narcissa Whitman and Elizabeth Spalding. Traveling west for their honeymoons, they had to discard their precious possessions one by one to lighten the load on the over-taxed animals. Finally they had to cut their covered wagon in half, and they reached Idaho in a rickety two-wheeled vehicle. They barely made it to Oregon on horseback. Six months after they arrived, Narcissa delivered the first white American child born west of the Continental Divide.[1]

Honeymoon Hideout

In contrast, the Genesis beginning was housed in perfection for Adam and Eve. Life was genial. First, let's pick up the weather report: *But a mist used to rise from the earth and water the whole surface of the ground (Genesis 2:6).*

The honeymoon cottage had an automatic sprinkler system!

It also had an eastern exposure. The morning sun came into the kitchen: *And the Lord God planted a garden toward the east, in Eden; and there He placed the man whom He had formed (Genesis 2:8).*

The job outlook was bright. Adam stayed busy with the creation: *And out of the ground the Lord God formed every beast of the field and every bird of the sky, and brought them to the man to see what he would call them; and whatever the man called a living creature, that was its name (Genesis 2:19).*

Eve had it made. She was even spared the pain of growing up. When God created her, she had everything she needed! Move in for a close-up view.

In the original Hebrew God used two different words to describe the creation of Adam and Eve. In creating the man, the ordinary word for "make" is used, such as one would describe the molding of a clay pot. In portraying Eve's appearance, however, the verb used means "hand-crafted," or, literally, "built." *And the Lord God fashioned* [built] *into a woman the rib which He had taken from the man, and brought her to the man (Genesis 2:22, NASB).*

A holy hush is noticeable over this event. It stands in sharp contrast to the coarseness and irreverence in which modern life is packaged. The silence seems to signify a historic fulcrum, for with Eve the pulse of humanity begins to beat. One can see it coming in the words of the Creator: *Then the Lord God said, "It is not good for the man to be alone; I will make him a helper suitable for him"* [corresponding to] *him (Genesis 2:18, NASB).* Jehovah spoke. It was the first time He had said anything was *not* good.

Morning of Purity

*J*ehovah God never wastes words, never indulges in idle prattle or useless thinking. There is no secondary level of importance to His communications. He spoke, and He said that it was not good that man should be alone.

Alone? With every animal on earth a personal friend, subject to his every whim, responsive to his commands? Alone? With God Himself coming to call?

Alone. Because he himself was incomplete, unfinished for God's purposes. A vacancy existed in his personal experience.

Notice that God did not make another man to fill the void. He did not need an apprentice in the garden, or a colleague to help catalog the animals. He was performing his job adequately. Adam was no underachiever; his need was singularly private.

Adam's lines of communication moved upward to his Maker and downward to the earthly plants and animals, but there was no reply to a horizontal message. He obviously noticed how each animal sent out its mating call—and received a response.

I remember touching the sensitive nerve of a common yearning deep inside myself and Howie before we were married. As engaged couples do, we discussed sex and marriage, future dreams all interlocked with the tidy idealism that erects castles in the air. My memory refuses to play back an exact recording of his statement, but he told me with high-voltage intensity how much he honored and respected and loved one person—me. That statement, now reinforced with almost a half-century of knowing him intimately, propelled me into a flight pattern in which I still soar. No other human experience quite equals the certainty that you are the one and only lifetime choice of your partner.

Adam, of course, did not make that choice; God made it for him. And I believe that God also made it for my husband, since we humans are not really smart enough to choose mates. One big reason is that we simply cannot see the future.

This man Adam was made to love another like himself, to share this Edenic life, to laugh, to dream, to find completeness in another person. Without Eve God's creation was not yet finished. He had crowned the magnificent progression of animal life with the making of a man, a unique creation fashioned on His own glory, made with the ability to know and understand something of the heart and mind of the eternal God. Now He would crown this man-reflection of Himself with yet another reflection.

Even as Adam portrayed God's glory in the earthly habitation, so this new creature would interpret Adam. She would provide the extension of Adam's self in sensitive paths where he could not go. She would make him a whole being; add to him the dimension of full, well-rounded satisfaction to his life. She would furnish the means to produce more individuals to populate the fresh new earth.

"Ugh! Eve was made from one of Adam's spare parts, almost as an afterthought to help him out on earth!" spewed one disgusted female.[2]

"God created woman...and from that moment boredom ceased. And many other things ceased as well. Woman was God's second mistake." So snorted Friedrich Wilhelm Nietzsche.[3]

Derailed, deluded modern man would discredit God's holy purpose. Is this narrative genuine? Is the creation story a fake, perpetrated on us by some clever old Jewish storyteller? We assume and rest our eternal destiny on the fact that these events really happened. A sparkling thread attesting authenticity spins into the precepts of Moses, the prophets, the evangelists' Scripture, even affirmed by Jesus Christ Himself. On through the teaching of the church fathers, the conclusions of precise deliberations by Sir Isaac Newton, and an innumerable host of others. Many valiant men, such as John Wycliffe and Alexander Solzhenitsyn, have staked their lives on the veracity of this Word.

Meanwhile, back in the garden, who was the new woman on the scene? Adam leaves his eyewitness account. God gave her the finest welcome any debutante ever had. When He brought her to the man, this brilliant intellect, this executive over the whole complex eco-system, he responded immediately, *"This is now bone of my bones, and flesh of my flesh; she shall be called 'Woman,' because she was taken out of Man" (Genesis 2:23).*

Identity

The first thing Eve received was identity. The Hebrew reads literally, *This one at this time.* Dr. Francis Schaeffer points out that this designation gave the historical emphasis.[4] The expression was one of excitement and enthusiasm, *Here now at last!* Jesus Christ confirmed the statement centuries later (Matthew 19:4). She was what she was because she was taken out of man. One man and one woman—a complete unit.

Relationship

I have been waiting for *you.* That is the thought behind Adam's initial words. What sweeter sound could she have heard? Not only does she learn that she is a full-fledged person, but she also shares a relationship. Adam observed that her bone and her flesh matched his own—physical compatibility. Not only did she match; she was part of him. He understood what God had done. No need to elaborate on the physiological kinship. Because she came from his body, she was special. He wanted to protect and provide for her.

Eve—God's Masterpiece

The Creator brought an orderly universe out of chaos. He set the stars and planets in motion, and adjusted the earth on its axis. He spoke light into being and limited the boundaries of the oceans, dressed the earth with living plant-life; all the earth teeming with swarms of winged and crawling creatures, four-footed beasts and numberless sea creatures, a myriad of living beings from micro-organisms to friendly mammals.

Then He scooped up dust from the ground, formed a man and breathed into him His heavenly breath; whereupon man became a living soul. The woman He brought was custom-fit for the man's need for beauty, for fun, for challenge, for fellowship; she was the imprint of the Almighty. God made Eve as the crowning jewel of His creative design. Not only did she complete the man, she became his emotional guardian, the maternal nurturer of all succeeding generations, the matriarch of the human race.

Eve needed Adam as much as he needed her, two intended to become one. The late Dr. Arthur Custance, a brilliant scientific researcher, wrote:

> I suggest that it is not a question of whether a man should be a bachelor or whether a woman should be a spinster but rather that neither a man nor a woman should be so self-sufficient as to feel no sense whatever of an incompleteness. We are in our relationships.[4]

Spiritual Suicide

The third chapter of Genesis clutches the reader with horror. Slithering up to the radiant woman with exotic grace, the serpent played his most beguiling tune, a ruinous refrain that would echo through the ages, destroying many souls: *Hath God Said?*

Eve—and history—turned a sharp corner in a flash. The serpent hissed and Eve inverted paradise. A mere question, quivering like the jab of a needle, pierced her innocence. She toppled helpless, unsuspecting before her enemy.

Scan the scene. She was apparently alone in the garden. With intellect, innocence and integrity intact, she was approached by a speaking animal. He had no business talking. He was by definition a beast of the field. All plant and animal life had been created to glorify God in their particular spheres (Psalm 19) and Adam had been put in charge to subdue them. His naming process was symbolic; in the Hebrew culture naming indicated authority or protectorship. Adam knew the creatures, named them and assumed responsibility for them. A beast of the field presuming to question the Creator was out of place. It appears to have been a blind spot for Eve.

Most important and obvious is the content of what the tempter said. His initial question was a challenge to the authority and integrity of the Creator. He asked about the one prohibition in God's plan for the man and woman. Because of his not-so-gentle persuasion, the woman committed an act of disobedience. It was an act to which she was not intellectually committed, but probably drawn by her essential nature. The consequence led to an indictment not only of herself but her human race.

After centuries of reflection, we, as descendants of this hapless pair, still stand aghast. How could it have happened? We still ask, yet we know because we ourselves are doing the same things every day.

Theologians may explain with philosophical finesse, but my female makeup wants to climb into Eve's thinking. It's not just curiosity; there's a key in there, a secret combination that will unlock my own stubborn savagery—that same puzzle of human nature Paul described: *...the good that I wish, I do not do; but I practice the very evil that I do not wish (Romans 7:19, NASB).*

The Curled Tongue

How cleverly worded was the query: Did God *really* say that you should not eat of a particular tree of the garden? The serpent (whose identity is not yet uncovered) knew quite well what God had said. He also knew that Eve knew, but knowledge must be skillfully employed; then it becomes wisdom. Eve knew the right facts, but the serpent understood how easily her thinking could be short-circuited. He assumed a similar thinking posture to hers.

Actually, it is an old salesman's trick, posed to create doubt. "Are you really satisfied with your automobile?" Naturally my car is not perfect in every respect. I am tempted to say, "Well, no not totally." And that admission of something less than perfection opens the door for further persuasion.

Honesty compelled Eve to explain there was one tree forbidden. Aha! An exception! Enough of an opening for the apparently curious inquirer to press his point. It intrigues me to observe that Eve misquoted God, adding that she should not touch it, lest she die.

God had not said anything about touching it. Was this Eve's interpretation? Not a bad one. Stay away. Don't flirt with trouble.

Another small mystery piques my thinking. The reference to a state that neither Adam nor Eve knew—death. Although it was out of the range of their experience God apparently had given them understanding beyond their immediate world. We do not have to experience something to understand it.

Words always rest on the virtue of the speaker. Talk is cheap, unless a man is as good as his word... and *...it is impossible for God to lie (Hebrews 6:18). What He had promised, He was able also to perform (Romans 4:21).*

39

My counsel shall stand (Isaiah 46:10). These are the words of Paul and of Isaiah. The psalmist sums it up, *Forever, O Lord, Your word is settled in heaven (Psalm 119:89).*

Then why did Eve allow the serpent to pursue the possibility that God did not mean what He said? Because the serpent was speaking in the framework of Satan, who was a liar from the beginning, according to Jesus (John 8:44). Dr. C. I. Scofield explains:

> Satan...as prince of this world system, is the real though unseen ruler of the successive world powers... (Isa. 14:13) The serpent in his Edenic form, is not to be thought of as a writhing reptile. That is the effect of the curse. The creature which lent itself to Satan may well have been the most beautiful as it was the most 'subtle' of creatures less than man. Traces of that beauty remain despite the curse....In the serpent Satan appeared as an angel of light.[5]

Was she simply a happy, frolicsome young woman, totally delighted by her home, fully unsuspecting—and unthinking? She did possess superior intelligence. She knew the answer. Talking with the serpent was certainly not wrong. Highly unusual, perhaps, but not disobedient—merely dangerous. Nevertheless, the consequences of that conversation were lethal.

The Manager

The terse biblical record states simply that she saw that the fruit was good for food. How womanly!

Something in our female heads wants to find things useful. We want flowers that bloom, clean water and accurate clocks. We want sharp knives and soft sheets, obedient children and understanding husbands, on-time paychecks and off-beat playtimes. The fruit was good for food, why not use it? Eve thought she spotted a good bargain!

The Beautician

When the seducer accosted the innocent woman she revealed another charming trait, her exquisite sensitivities. Was the fruit still on the vine, providing a brilliantly appealing ensemble, or had he coaxed her to pick one and just hold the flawless piece of fresh produce in her hand? Whatever the case, it was pleasing to her senses. Perhaps it exuded a lovely aroma; it may have felt soft or smooth to the touch. It was *pleasing to the eye* (Genesis 3:6), a moment of sensual luxury for Eve.

Throughout history beauty has been associated with women. The scriptures report clearly that Sarah, Abraham's wife, was very beautiful. When Abraham's servant set out to find a wife for his master's son Isaac, he found Rebekah, who was also very beautiful. Isaac's son Jacob loved his wife Rachel because of her beauty.

Queen Esther won the heart of the powerful Medo-Persian King Xerxes because of her refined loveliness. The bent toward beauty appears to be a built-in tendency, created by God such that since the Fall His warnings appear in both Old and New Testaments. Proverbs closes with this caution:

Charm is deceptive, and beauty is fleeting; but a woman who fears the Lord is to be praised (Proverbs 31:30).

The apostle Peter, writing to believers, assures them of God's desire for integrated beauty throughout a woman's whole being:

Your beauty should not come from outward adornment, such as braided hair and the wearing of gold jewelry and fine clothes. Instead it should be that of your inner self, the unfading beauty of a gentle and quiet spirit, which is of great worth in God's sight (I Peter 3:3,4, NIV).

Dr. Joe Aldrich comments:

Beauty as a concept is not easy to define. It is part of the same family with truth, love, life, reality and holiness. These concepts are so closely tied together that one cannot speak of one without touching the other.[6]

Eve herself undoubtedly reflected her Maker's divine beauty, and quite likely the resplendent fruit captured her natural passion for splendor.

The Investigator

Curiosity, the third aspect of the woman's winsomeness, lured her into a new dimension. With the words *desirable* for *gaining wisdom* Eve's penchant for wanting to be in the know leaped to the fore. The serpent suggested that God was withholding a kernel of know-how, and that proposal dissolved any remaining inhibition.

The master deceiver knew better than to slap on her a harsh contradiction of divine order. Instead he jacked up his proposition with seemingly logical reasoning. *You will not surely die. For God knows that when you eat of it your eyes will be opened, and you will be like God, knowing good and evil (Genesis 3:4-5).* A direct denial, but sugar-coated with an appeal to status and knowledge.

Mm-mmm! She was no idiot. She listened, considered, and with womanly instinct decided at least to take a look. Did she, perhaps, have a vague foreboding that mystified and intrigued her? Could she have felt impish and impetuous? Or was she so focused that she ignored the flashing red lights?

What the serpent said was partially true. She would know good and evil. Wow! How exciting! You can almost see the goose bumps pop up as she gets ready to take a first-time joyride. Sadly, Eve did not realize that she had no capacity to handle evil.

Just think, a new food! Its luster and shape and fragrance! And now the prospect of gaining wisdom drew her strangely toward it. With the insistent prodding of history's most wicked double-cross, she doubted...she denied...she disobeyed...and she destroyed her innocence, jeopardizing her husband and all her future children.

Blinded by the dazzle of that lightning flash, she failed to take into account the whole picture. She based her actions upon very superficial evidence. She did not stop to throw upon the screen of her judgment the two contrasting testimonies: *If you eat, you shall die!* and *You will not surely die!*

Moreover, as a team member she should have consulted Adam; but she was, as are her daughters centuries removed, free to make her own decisions, free to ignore what she knew was right, free to act without really thinking, but never free to escape entrapment, to sidestep the consequences of disobedience.

Eve spoke...saw...ate...gave. The New Testament comments on this episode with taciturn reflection: *...the woman being quite deceived, fell into transgression (1 Timothy 2:14).*

She was not tempted because she was evil; but because she was human. Part of that humanity was an insatiable desire for knowledge. The decision dangled on a small piece of fruit, but the consequences hatched seeds of destruction for every child yet to be born.

The Moment of Truth

∾

Can you possibly imagine the dread of listening for the voice of God? Adam and Eve had often revelled in God's words, but now it was different. They each had a guilty conscience. Little wonder that Adam says, *I heard the sound of Thee in the garden and I was afraid because I was naked; and I hid myself (Genesis 3:10).*

He was afraid not because God is by nature angry and vindictive. It was not the fear of the prisoner for the harsh jailer, but the debilitating guilt of one who has defaulted in the face of beauty, freedom, love and generosity.

Where are you? God asked. Adam used his nakedness to defend his disappearance. How absurd! God had created him unclothed. He explained very carefully before the serpent ever danced onto the stage that *the man and his wife were both naked and were not ashamed (Genesis 2:25, NASB).* After disobeying, *Then*

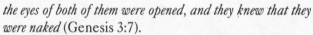

the eyes of both of them were opened, and they knew that they were naked (Genesis 3:7).

Note that it was after they ate the fruit that their eyes were opened. Dr. Edward J. Young comments:

> It is not of the physical eyes that the Scripture speaks here, when it states that their eyes were 'opened' for Adam and Eve had not been physically blind. ...Rather the reference is to the arousing of the conscience and an awakening of the understanding so that the man and the woman now see themselves in a tragic condition and seek deliverance therefrom.[7]

Perhaps cold winds blew and clouds covered the couple shivering in their makeshift fig-leaf tunics. Spiritual death had already started to deteriorate the now-sinful couple, with shame and guilt as a part of that death status. Is the instinctive need to cover our bodies a visual aid of the need for shrouding our guilt? I think so. Does it follow then, that the ability to ignore that self-conscience is a healthy victory? Obviously not. Nakedness in the Bible is always related to poverty, shame or helplessness. Christ's words, *I was naked and you clothed me (Matthew 25:36)* illustrate that He regards lack of clothing to be a sign of humiliation. Job reminds us of the defenselessness: ...*naked I came from my mother's womb, and naked I shall return there (Job 1:21).*

God sees us as we are but gives us promise that not even nakedness shall separate us from the love of God (Romans 8:35). He Himself provided the first wardrobe from animal skins, an evidence of His mercy and loving kindness.

Our day-to-day Christian guidelines must include modesty. Standards vary, but common sense and the guiding presence of the Spirit within leads me to know what's right for us. He gives a sense of propriety—not the current issue of *Women's Wear Daily*.

Don't Blame Me!

God refused to allow His interrogation to be detoured. He moved right to the issue at hand. *Have you eaten from the tree of which I commanded you not to eat (Genesis 3:11)?*

Here was Adam's first opportunity to tell the truth, to ask for forgiveness. Instead he gave an excuse. In the showdown before the Almighty, Adam blamed his wife for his actions. You can almost see the beads of perspiration on his brow as he fidgeted and pointed a finger at Eve. *The woman whom Thou gavest to be with me, she gave me from the tree, and I ate* (Genesis 3:12).

He put the blame indirectly on God. *You really cannot blame me. It was her idea—and she was your idea—and I just went along with her.*

In a distorted sense it was true; but he as leader was responsible and it was on him that God placed primary blame. Paul's New Testament comment explains, *For it was Adam who was first created and then Eve, and it was not Adam who was deceived... (1 Timothy 2:13-14).*

Knowing fully his rash disobedience, Adam was required to name his sin. His weak, pass-the-buck reply did even merit a divine response. God then quizzed Eve: culpable, responsible for her own actions. She pointed her finger at the serpent.

Parents often witness this kind of lame reasoning with children. Sister comes home dragging dirty little brother. Questioning ends up with *I couldn't help it—he wanted to walk on the curb, and the car came by...* Excuses; they began with the Fall.

Since Adam and Eve are our ancestors and our co-defendants before the bar of God's justice, we try to vindicate them. The circumstantial evidence needs to be heard, we protest. Besides, couldn't God overlook a little mistake, a harmless first offense? We try to rewrite it like a nursery rhyme. Eve fell down and broke her crown and Adam came tumbling after. So why can't you just pick yourself up and promise to be more careful next time?

The problem is there's a war on. A spiritual conflict. The serpent was simply a front for the real villain. Something catastrophic happened before Eden. Isaiah the prophet opens the attic closet and shows us the skeleton, *How you are fallen from heaven, O Lucifer, son of the morning...You have said in your heart: I will ascend into heaven, I will exalt my throne above the stars of God...I will be like the Most High (Isaiah 14:12-14).* Eve was simply the first human victim. Satan (Lucifer) had declared eternal war against God, and this was the first recorded skirmish. This explains why Jehovah God wrote the bottom line in bold black ink. We call it *The Curse.*

Note however, that only the serpent and the ground were cursed. Adam and Eve received separate rebukes and prophetic messages. *To the woman, I will greatly multiply your sorrow and your conception, in pain you shall bring forth children; your desire shall be for your husband, and he shall rule over you (Genesis 3:16).*

These words closed Eve's honeymoon. She was like a house damaged in a storm. The parts were there, but in disarray. Her innocence was gone because she had exercised her free will to disobey her Creator. God relocated Adam and Eve outside the garden, away from the tree of life, an act of grace to prevent their living in misery forever. There she would begin a harsh uphill battle adjusting to the life she had chosen, one of independence from God.

The High Cost of Living Outside Eden

❧

*G*ood morning, world! Guess what? There is a lilt of triumph in Eve's greeting as she cries out in the first verse of Genesis 4, *I have gotten a manchild with the help of the Lord.* A tiny, helpless man-child. The only other person in the world had been a man—her brilliant, gifted partner-husband. Now there was a third and her heart sang out loud.

Many of us have shared the shining moment of her joy. The hope of a bright future comes at that first sight of the newborn child so exquisitely formed, utterly tender and innocent, and he is *mine*. A little Cain followed his father in learning the pursuit of agriculture.

Then another son—Abel. Joy, exultation, thanksgiving. Love poured out to these sons. But the record does not satisfy our rubbernecking nature about the human factors that added up to produce the first family explosion, the sibling rivalry, the murder.

What estrangement was there between Adam and Eve? Were there times when Eve, heavy with child and haunted by her past indiscretion, ached for Adam to hold her close—and he was lost in his own world, fighting with the fields to get crops to grow? Did they argue over whose fault this mess was? On one issue they agreed: the source of her precious babies was God Himself, but little did she realize that Adam's seed, implanted in those new lives, was a time bomb of personal disaster.

Parenthood was then, as it is now, a precarious profession. Balancing indulgence with limitation is a feat that requires supernatural wisdom. Love can sometimes blur our vision. Was Cain, like Jacob, a "mama's boy" who got his own way, or had too much too soon? Or was Adam so resentful about being evicted from the garden that he was too rigid and harsh, causing Cain to rebel? Eve was learning what the Lord meant by sorrow and pain with children.

New babies have always inspired hope; one more divine opportunity to start over, perhaps to do better than before. Having lived in the concealed safety of his mother's body, the newborn is ushered into the harsh brilliance of strange surroundings, wanting nothing more than closeness and comfort from his mother—her touch, her milk, her voice. His fledgling innocence knows nothing of her tainted soul, her maternal gifts flawed with strains of selfishness.

It was so with Eve on those bright birthdays of Cain and Abel, and every subsequent nativity plays a variation on this wildcat theme. One is hard-pressed to predict what the presence of this child will do to a mother in her up-and-down world of hectic schedules, chance happenings and erratic harmonies. The dark diary of that first family has been kept secret, but the startling headlines of manslaughter have tormented the world throughout history.

Night of Terror

Biblical names always suggest the purpose and often a prophecy for their owners. Cain means "acquisition," Abel conveys "that which ascends." The first seemed to be pulling everything down to himself, while the other is sending everything up. They were indeed opposites.

Domestic details are missing, but we cannot escape the blowout: *Cain rose up against Abel his brother and killed him (Genesis 4:8).* How can that be? It's incredible. We knock on the door of our friend Eve to ask some questions. Eve's spirit is devastated. Her announcement that the family had expanded to three, and four, has been deflated. The divine words spoken after her crushing serpent episode had dulled somewhat. But now they are pulsing like a raging fever in her brain. *In pain you shall bring forth children...* Pain. So this was part of the price tag. That fresh grave—that peculiar ache of knowing your criminal son is wandering and you do not know where...

The Crippled Caregiver

I suspect that a thousand questions anchored that first beautiful woman to an emotional valley. Had she overindulged? How had they failed as parents? Why hadn't she sensed the incompatibility and somehow intervened? Was Cain, after all, more like his mother? Why did she listen to that serpent and ruin everything? Tragedy is hard enough to endure by yourself, but having to watch your child go though it is indescribable agony.

Dr. Roy Zuck, in the compelling saga of his daughter's injury and recovery from a near-fatal auto accident, expressed vividly his own feelings in a chapter entitled, "The Long Saturday."

> Like giant rats, those questions began to gnaw at my mind. But I kept them to myself, not wanting to add to Dottie's fear. And yet I realized she was probably thinking similar questions.[8]

Shock, grief, exhaustion and then inevitably the slow, painful process of analysis. What are the cold facts in the light of a new day?

It all centered on the sacrifice situation. God had slain animals and used the skins for clothing. Instructions had obviously been given; the symbolic death of animals atoned for offenses against God's Holy Person, foreshadowing the perfect Person who was to come and die for the sin of man. Henceforth, animals were to be slain as sacrifices for sin.

Sacrifice is bloody. Who wants to kill a lovable, healthy little lamb that never hurt anything? But God had commanded it. It was a matter of obedience to authority. Not that again! Yes, the same song, second generation.

Satan had scored a hit against God's appointed mother of humanity. *And Adam called his wife's name Eve, because she was the mother of all living (Genesis 3:20).* Nurturing was part of Eve's nature. She stands as the prototype for every succeeding mother. Because she cares so much, enthralling joy and punishing disappointment are parts of the package, but her mother's heart outlasts it all.

The Would-Be Governor

With the divine pronouncement, *Your desire shall be for your husband, and he shall rule over you (Genesis 3:16),* future frustrations were assigned for every woman. Just as Eve's inborn need to nurture would bring sorrow because of her waywardness, so her strong tendency to fight for power would get thwarted by the man, generating distance between the sexes.

The thought behind the desire for her husband is that of influencing him according to her will. Just as she had given him the forbidden fruit, her daughters after her would try to manipulate their men. But God said the men would be the ultimate masters. What a dire predicament!

Remember how the relationship started: *For this cause a man shall leave his father and his mother, and shall cleave to his wife; and they shall become one flesh (Genesis 2:24).* In a flash of brilliant insight, the first man understood the Creator's purpose and set the course of sociology. A tripartite pronouncement: Man was to break a relationship he himself had not experienced (parent-child) to form a new unit of society, and to engage in a unique blend of interpersonal mating. One person plus one person equals one person.

All the pleasant, stimulating botanical and zoological studies that Adam had enjoyed—even the marvelous communion with God Himself—could not do for the man what this woman could. Adam must have looked at her from head to toe, talked with her, and bubbled over in a crescendo of joy. There is no hint of a foreboding *(Now my troubles are beginning)* or that he suspected God had subtly foisted a burden on him. Eve was not an additional job assignment; he understood clearly and was elated. She had made him complete.

So God created a married couple. Interesting, isn't it? The holy state of matrimony, trampled and degraded in man's schemes, glistens at the peak of the perfect creation. One can only imagine the marvelous details of their wedded bliss. Did God whisper any premarital instructions to Eve? How did he prepare her for wife-hood? We cannot know all the delicate inner lining of Eve's early bliss, but we do know she flourished in a union legally sanctioned and secured by the Judge of all the universe.

On this historical basis I, Eve's daughter, can place my own identity. I know who I am, and how I am made—in the image of God. That fact gives me reverence and respect for my body, my mind, and a cue for my eternal destiny. It tells me God is all-wise, all-powerful and all-loving. As I learn to know Him, I can reach out to others. My life has meaning and purpose.

Eve in Custody

We must ask the question, why did Adam, so wise and rational, comply with Eve's suggestion to sin? I believe he may have feared separation from his beloved beauty. By himself he probably would never have stooped to such a dialogue as Eve had; that is why the serpent accosted her. But Adam did not love the serpent as he loved Eve. Every loved wife knows she has hidden power to bend her husband's will in her direction. When *Eve* offered the forbidden fruit, Adam ate it.

In His wisdom God placed Eve under the protectorship of her husband. Like a beautiful thoroughbred mare, she had to be carefully guarded—not because her owner is trying to punish her, but to safeguard her purity, to shield her from the eager stallions who would defile her. She has spirit and capability; she is in every way equal to her male counterpart. Perhaps she could even beat him in a race. Her very potential makes her a prize to be sheltered.

The Fall, the harsh sledgehammer of sin, wounded Eve's love life. Few daily clippings find their way to the pages of the Bible, but always we see the results of alienation in the deceit and unfaithfulness found in the lives of subsequent families. Eve wanted to take charge of her life, to make her own decisions, to be her own person, but she walked into a trap. More than that, she demoted her husband along with herself and poisoned the souls of all who come after her. God did not change her leaning toward leadership; He merely placed her in protective custody with His means of regeneration available.

Part Two

HOW DOES SHE FUNCTION?

THE JEWEL
God's highest purpose for His beloved daughters lies in her exquisite capability to reproduce herself in other lives, an infiltration of love and goodness to men, and a tutor of what is best in life for children and other women.

THE MANAGER
Normal impulses provoke a woman to organize and nail down her personal life. Under divine control she is stunningly effective at pacing, balancing and stabilizing her world.

THE BEAUTICIAN
Deeply touched by her senses, a woman tends to act in response to what she perceives from her sensory guidance system.

THE INVESTIGATOR
Fear and natural inhibitions are overridden by a woman's insistent drive to discover additional details which could be of use to her.

THE CAREGIVER
All of the feminine leanings toward stability, gracefulness and inquisitiveness seem to converge into a natural ability to provide personal attention to anyone in need.

THE CONTROLLER
The opposite gender always presents a challenge to the female psyche. Instinctively she covets the opportunity to outwit him, but unless he is supernaturally disposed to regard her with respect she loses equality.

Finding the Jewel

ome years ago while visiting Breckenridge, Colorado, I read the story of an early Methodist preacher who had come to bring the gospel to the hard-nosed fortune-hunters of that silver mining town. As winter worsened and loneliness grew, the men began drinking to excess and building hostility toward the minister. Late one night they woke him with taunts outside his little hut, shouting for him to come out and preach to them. When he ignored them, they broke down the door and dragged him out, hoisting him onto a stump and jeering. As the good man surveyed the horde of carousers, he knew that any sermon he might attempt would only invite dishonor to God, so he appealed to their inflamed imaginations.

"Look over there, boys," he yelled. "A' comin' down the hill! Don't you see 'em? Pretty ladies! Why here they come up close. Jes' look at 'em—there's your little sister and your mama—" He went on to paint a word picture in their head as the bleary-eyed revelers blinked and stared. "And d'ya hear what they's a'saying?" Then, one by one he called out their names, and intoned what shame and disappointment these women were expressing, what tears they were shedding, as they saw the debauchery of their loved ones.

Slowly the crowd quieted and backed off. One by one they slinked away. The mere thought of a good woman brought an end to their mischief. Even in a morally corrupt world something of God's original plan and purpose for women still stands.

Vision of the Almighty

How did God intend feminine presence to function? We can discover that intention only by a careful look at those first primeval records—what Adam said, what God did and what He communicated. Our first view of bliss in Eden watched the unfolding of togetherness. God made a lone man who found his completeness in the gift of Eve, the woman God created from Adam's own human body.

To highlight the importance of the woman, look again at God's creation of man.

> *Then God said, "Let us make man in our image, in our likeness, and let them rule over the fish of the sea, and the birds of the air, over the livestock, over all the creatures that move along the ground. So God created man in his own image, in the image of God He created him; male and female He created them (Genesis 1:26-27, NIV).*

Dr. Stephen B. Clark comments:

> The human race was created last, the high point of the visible creation...to have dominion over the living things of the earth, and to increase and multiply...God, then, created humans to be like him...so that they could be his representatives and rule over part of creation.[9]

The divine purpose was to create a race of people to reflect His character of wisdom and love, bringing glory to God alone. Eve was His finishing touch; she added a reflection of God Himself with a unique luster of loveliness wholly her own. Her high calling, however, was to bring children into the world and, with her husband, anchor their young lives with cords of love strong enough to enable the next generation to begin.

The model of commitment, that a man should "cleave to his wife" and "become one flesh," becomes the paragon for the future human race. Eve is blessed with a secure love relationship and a clear objective for her life.

When Eve dealt in disobedience with the serpent and led her husband also to sin, God not only sought out the couple and provided covering for their cowering guilt, but he carefully explained to them the consequences of what they had done. His purpose would not be thwarted, but they would face insurmountable weakness without His enablement. Eve would continue as Adam's wife; she would indeed be the mother of the human race, but against odds too great for her.

The pain and servility could not be overcome without divine intervention.

Despite the sin nature, marriage reflects God's protective plan for women and mirrors His Son as the bridegroom loving the church. Paul's words to husbands highlight the value of wives:

> *Husbands, love your wives, just as Christ loved the church and gave himself up for her to make her holy, cleansing her by the washing with water through the word, and to present her to himself as a radiant church, without stain or wrinkle or any other blemish, but holy and blameless (Ephesians 5:25-27, NIV).*

As women, you and I are so important to God that He finds a way for us to enjoy restoration. Obviously in heaven we shall know freedom from the weaknesses of our corrupted fleshly natures, but meanwhile here on earth we have a formula for fulfillment.

A story is told of legendary department store merchant Bruce Nordstrom's concern for his customers. It seems he overheard two women shaking their heads in disappointment in one of his stores and asked his general manager to find out the problem. The manager inquired of the two, telling them how upset Mr. Nordstrom was at their displeasure. She discovered that the difficulty lay in the fact that they had seen dresses they liked very much in the Gallery, the expensive department, but could not afford the prices. As it happened, the manager was able to take them to the moderately priced department and find very similar dresses. The women were not only able to achieve their shopping goals, but they were ecstatic to know that the store owner cared. The manager was left with an indelible memory of a boss who was clear about his values and exemplified them in dealing with his customers.

Like those customers, we women want the best in life, but because of the sin in Eden, we are born without the moral equity to attain it. We make wrong decisions. Our Heavenly Father, however , who cares for us, makes it possible to find fulfillment, to be the woman He meant for us to be. He wants to unearth the jewel He created.

The sacrifice of His Son makes it possible. His life transforming our lives enables us to gain the rewards He intended. If we take seriously God's stellar role for a woman, we will use every inborn instinct to imitate the God of love and fulfill His expectations.

The Manager

We have already seen how Eve's efforts to organize Eden resulted in overriding the controls God had put in place. It was as if she climbed in the cockpit and assumed the pilot's place without a license. She cut the power, lowered the flaps and started a descent that turned into an out-of-control spin. Having lost first her lovely home, then her two beloved sons, she must have truly felt that she had crashed and burned. Only a glimmer of hope burns at the end of that dark fourth chapter of Genesis. There the reader learns that God gave Adam and Eve a replacement son, Seth, who had a son, Enos. At that time men began to call upon the name of the Lord (Genesis 4:26).

Underground Operation

After Eve the annals of biblical history go silent with regard to women. What happened in the homes of Eve's granddaughters and great-granddaughters? As the generations passed, we can only guess their fate. Clearly a godly line of men emerged, but the grim notation comes that the daughters of men were beautiful (Genesis 6:2) and were apparently exploited:

> *The Lord was grieved that he had made man on the earth, and his heart was filled with pain (Genesis 6:6, NIV).*

A cosmic catastrophe occurred. At God's command a great flood destroyed the beautiful earth, taking with it every creature in which God had breathed the breath of life. Only one family of eight souls escaped. In obedience to His command, Noah built an ark to protect his wife, his three sons and their wives from the forty-day disaster. Once more God demonstrated His saving grace.

Family on the Move

Generations continued with widespread dishonor to God until Abraham, a descendent of Shem, Noah's oldest son, married his half-sister, Sarai, in the great city of Ur. Sarai is the first woman named and profiled since Eve. In our frame of reference, this occurred in the Bronze Age near the Fertile Crescent.

> (Ur) was a leading Sumerian city, possessed an elaborate system of writing, advanced means of mathematical, astronomical and astrological computation, a mature and comprehensive religious organization, highly developed business and commercial procedures, a form of art, a flourishing educational system and other marks of a cultured society.[10]

From Ur the family migrated hundreds of miles northwesterly along the Euphrates River. How much did Sarai dread this nomadic life? Did she understand that, if there had to be a choice, a good relationship with her husband was far more important than a comfortable home? How much choice did she have? Her 75-year-old husband had received God's direction and His promise of blessing. Together they moved with all their cattle, servants and goods. They had only Abram's faith in Jehovah to lead the way.

Sarai enjoyed two assets: wealth and beauty. Besides being the wife of a shrewd and prosperous herdsman-administrator, she was also strikingly fair, a fact which occasioned her panic-stricken husband to lie twice to kings about his relationship in order to save himself. She was greatly respected and loved, an enviable position for any wife.

One persistent problem clouded her life. It drops with thud on the reader: *Sarai was barren; she had no child (Genesis 11:30).* Such a curse can barely be appreciated in our day, but for her its sad implications of silent shame can hardly be over-emphasized. Still Abram, trusting God for a son, never voluntarily took another wife while Sarai lived.

The long circuitous journey brought much anxiety. Consider the flight to Egypt, when Abram's faith was not strong enough to trust God for survival in famine-stricken Canaan. There Sarai willingly conspired with him to pose as his sister in order to save his life. Humanly such deception was logical, for common oriental practice condoned killing a man to gain his beautiful wife for the harem. Because Abram and Sarai had not been led by God to go to Egypt, it was with inner tension that they presented themselves to the monarch and lied to him.

Together they made their pact to deceive. Their faith was still a slender thread. It is only after trials and triumphs that faith grows and toughens in we weak humans. Once a sin is committed, how easy it is to do it again. Years later this same couple again reverted to their old behavior when a similar instance arose.

Horrified at the fiery downfall of Sodom, they fled the scene and were again faced by a powerful king, Abimilech. Again they dragged out their secondhand fraud, *He is my brother...(Genesis 20:5)*. They risked the purity of the promised seed as well as her chastity, dishonoring God and demonstrating that even a seasoned servant of Jehovah is subject to weakness and temptation.

Sarah's Plan to Solve God's Problem

During the stay in Egypt Sarai acquired a handmaiden named Hagar. She had taken the girl away from her Egyptian family and advanced civilization to go to an unsettled land. Hagar's family was obviously poor; Sarai was a favorite in the pharaoh's palace... Who would tell her no? Hagar left her home, probably willingly, and became the personal slave of the beautiful and rich Sarai.

Dr. Alexander Whyte of Scotland wrote:

As time went on, and as the hope of any possibility of her ever becoming a mother died out in

Sarah's heart, ...her terrible cross had but inflamed her to find some wild and willful way for herself to live any longer such an embarrassment to her husband, such an evident obstacle to the prosperity of his house, and such an eyesore and jest to all the camp and to all the country around.[11]

Time, distance and discouragement uncovered Sarai's manipulative qualities. With the soft pad of her paw she motioned Hagar to take her place, to have Abram's baby, to solve God's problem. How utterly foolish to think we can tell God how to do it! Then, caught in the net of her own design, frustrated by Hagar's insolence, Sarai dealt out harsh punishment and her slave ran away.

Sarai bared her claws. The gentle, beautiful Sarai turned beast! We have no right to criticize. Which of us has not hurt an innocent person to save our own reputation and to cover our own stupid mistakes? God's respectful dealing with Hagar is a salve for every disillusioned girl who has been used and misused by our insensitive society. How many are caught in the clutches of the rich and powerful, made slaves, only to be pitilessly thrown aside when they become a burden?

An angel confronted Hagar (Genesis 16) with two questions to bring her to her senses: Where did you come from? Where are you going? To the first she truthfully replied: *I am fleeing from the presence of my mistress Sarai.* To the second question she had no answer.

Return to your mistress, and submit yourself to her authority, the angel commanded. Never does God condone insubordination. With the rebuke came a promise: Her son would be called Ishmael, father of a great nation, a wild and warlike man.

With Ishmael's birth Abram began to see this boy as the promised son, but he had not yet learned that God means *exactly* what He says. Four years later, when Abram was ninety-nine years old, God again confirmed His promise and changed his name. No longer would he be Abram, but Abraham; not just "exalted father" but "father of a multitude."

Likewise, Sarai was to become Sarah, literally "princess." God was giving birth to a new nation and He was proclaiming royal status for its progenitors. Sarah, He promised, would bear a son.

Then Abraham fell on his face and laughed, and said in his heart, Will a child be born to a man one hundred years old? And will Sarah who is ninety years old, bear a child (Genesis 17:17, NIV)?

Incredible! But God again repeated the promise and gave to Abraham the name for his son, Isaac.

God Makes Good His Promise

Not long after that, God moved upon His word. Abraham spotted three men approaching his tent at midday. With characteristic hospitality he ran to welcome them, washed their feet, and offered refreshment. As was the custom, the men ate together while Sarah stood apart behind the tent door. *Where is Sarah?* they asked. *In the tent,* answered the host.

I will certainly return to you at this time next year, and Sarah your wife shall have a son. Now it was Sarah's turn to laugh. Not aloud, but within herself. The angel heard. *Why did Sarah laugh? Is anything too difficult for the Lord?...Sarah shall have a son (Genesis 18:13-14, NIV).*

Sarah, embarrassed for laughing and caught lying again, took giant strides in her development of believing God's word. Perhaps the question rang over and over again in her mind: *Is anything too hard for the Lord (Genesis 18:14, NIV)?*

Having announced the impending birth, the angels departed toward Sodom to announce impending death. Sarah's life had been a series of supernatural deliverances, divine victories and demonstrations of God's power in the midst of idolatrous and wicked people. Then at Gerar she witnessed the amazing disentanglement from the hand of Abimilech. She was finally convinced God could do what He said. She would not deny His word. She had to believe; there was no other solution to the problem. If God did not miraculously provide the baby, there would be no child. She believed the impossible for herself and God honored her faith. It took ninety years of preparation.

Birth Announcement

Unprecedented rejoicing came to the tent of Abraham with the birth of Isaac. Any birth evoked joy but this miracle was a special proof of God's reliability. When Isaac was weaned at the age of three, Abraham made a great feast. Never before had the family known such a celebration.

Watching from the wings with jealous eyes were Ishmael and his mother, Hagar. Again there was rudeness, mocking and envy. Again Sarah reacted with anger, asking Abraham to cast them both out of her home.

Abraham's tender nature recoiled at the thought of such severe treatment. He had come to love his son Ishmael. Yet God Himself affirmed Sarah's judgment... *"Listen to her, for through Isaac your descendants shall be named" (Genesis 21:12, NIV).*

Once more Hagar was alone in the wilderness and once more in her hour of extremity she was confronted by the voice of God. *What is the matter with you Hagar? Do not fear... (Genesis 21:17, NIV).* Miraculously He provided water and sustenance for Hagar and Ishmael. Life went on, and the record notes that Hagar procured a wife from Egypt for her son, taking him back home to meet the family.

Sarah lived to be 127 years old. Her death and burial are recorded, the only woman so immortalized in the Scriptures. We can readily see why God weaves this woman in the exquisite tapestries of the New Testament, too. She was married to a man with a rare aptitude for believing God and she learned from him. The secret of faith came first by practicing obedience. By nature she was the model manager, thinking her way through life, but only mixed with faith does the manager please God.

In two instances she is singled out in the New Testament for special commendation. Those two medals of honor form the key to unlocking her secret of success. The first: *She obeyed her husband.*

In the same way, you wives, be submissive to your own husbands so that even if any of them are disobedient to the word, they may be won without a word by the behavior of their wives, as they observe your chaste and respectful behavior...For in this way in former times the holy women also, who hoped in God, used to adorn themselves, being submissive to their own husbands. Thus Sarah obeyed Abraham, calling him lord, and you have become her children if you do what is right without being frightened by any fear (1 Peter 3:1-6, NASB).

The second citation: *She believed what God had promised.*

By faith even Sarah herself received ability to conceive, even beyond the proper time of life, since she considered Him faithful who had promised (Hebrews 11:11, NASB).

Management by Divine Dependence

Eve saw that the fruit was good for food; thus Sarah, her daughter, quite naturally devised an alternative to God's promise. Each one suffered for acting on her human impulse to set circumstances in order. Must we conclude that management skills are dangerous and sinful? Not at all. But operating under God's direction is the only way to avoid disillusionment.

Recent studies in America show that clinical depression ranks second only to advanced coronary disease in the total number of days patients spend in the hospital or disabled at home. Days lost from work among those who receive no treatment is estimated at upwards of $12 billion, and the individuals are plagued with poor concentration, faulty memory, fatigue, apathy, a lack of confidence and debilitating indecisiveness.

How much of our serious enfeeblement stems from repeated attempts to make our lives work without supernatural help? And when life doesn't work, how many sink into the mire of self-pity and despair?

The Beautician

⚜

*W*hen it comes to looking good, smelling sweet, sounding and feeling just right, we women move to front and center. It was so with wise and lovely Abigail; she rose to the top from an unlikely pit of marital failure. Mismatched marriages are grist for the mills of movies, novels and gossip columns. Pop psychology pundits advise bewildered wives to "get rid of the bum," and the public enjoys the spectacle. But in real life a wife on the bottom of a lopsided marriage suffers beyond description. For the partner who is committed to keeping the marriage vows, life with a chronic loser brings continual pain like nothing else, an unseen domestic violence. One counselor wrote:

> Physical and mental exhaustion are even more common than anxiety and insomnia in abused women. They feel drained and numb...They stop thinking about the future and become

chronically depressed. In one clinical study of 100 battered women, 42 had attempted suicide.[13]

Clean-up Chore

The Old Testament world during the early days of Israel held an aching similarity to our own. As if to highlight what daily life was like, the Bible related the narrative of Abigail (1 Samuel 25). It does not say that she was a battered wife, nor abused physically in any way, but she teaches us a valuable lesson about the joy of living and hope for the future, even though she was under the thumb of her stingy husband. It is a nugget of truth that raises true beauty to sparkling brilliance against a sordid background.

Backdrop for Bad Times

Abigail, wife of the all-time loser, Nabal, demonstrated what a woman can do in a humanly hopeless marriage. Undoubtedly, the Nabal-Abigail wedding was arranged—all marriages in that day were. No detail on family circumstances is given; all we know is that an admirable and praiseworthy woman was married to a roughneck rogue. What a shame! Our sympathies are with her, but consolation does not solve the problem. Apparently her whole household pitied her, but feeling sorry could not change her circumstances. Abigail's fuel for igniting change lay deeper within herself. That same power remains for us today.

Abigail's home was probably isolated, as sheepherders' often were. Dealing in the indispensable wool market, Nabal earned sizable profits. Wealth and success, however, did not wear well on him. He was an early day Scrooge, "surly and mean in his dealings."

His stingy nature extended beyond business to other people. He was inconsiderate to his servants, ill-informed about his own government and indifferent to any social obligations. Nabal personified God's description of a fool:

A worthless person, a wicked man,
Walks with a perverse mouth;...
He devises evil continually,
He sows discord (Proverbs 6:12-14).

Go from the presence of a foolish man...The house of
the wicked will be overthrown...There is a way that
seems right to a man, but its end is the way of death
(Proverbs 14:7,11,12).

Close-Up of a Commendable Wife

In contrast Abigail steps on to the biblical page with a favorable introduction. *She was an intelligent and beautiful woman.* Every woman wants to be known for these two qualities, but imagine receiving such approval from God Himself! For all eternity she is praised in the Book that will never go out of print and enjoys worldwide circulation. But why this assessment of Abigail?

Many mistreated and unloved wives are blinded by their misery and hot desire for revenge. They

waste energy on denying the truth instead of building
on the promises of the Creator. Abigail understood
how she fit into God's family and she knew God
alone could rescue her. She apparently waited for His
deliverance, keeping herself alert and ready.

Nabal's final act opened at sheep-shearing time on
the ranch; a season of intense labor, but also one of
celebration for the harvest. By custom, good will was
extended to all, much as in our modern Christmas
season. In Nabal's community, however, the sobering
reality was that thievery also abounded at this time.
When the workers were busy shearing, roving robbers
(or wild animals) often vandalized; sheep-shearing
was a period of vulnerability. With every ranch hand
needed for the wool harvest, few men were available
for guard duty.

Royalty in Training

During this shearing, which may have lasted for
some weeks, David, who had already been anointed
the future king, was hiding out from King Saul in
Nabal's neighborhood. He had his own band of loyal
mercenaries. Though this group could have caused
problems by stealing, they did not. They acted as
protectors, not vandals. David maintained strict disci-
pline and a code of ethical conduct. In accordance
with local custom, he sent ten of his men to call on
Nabal. In effect, they said, "Greetings of the season!
We are your neighbors and would like to join you for
your celebration feast."

Without firm property rights and boundary lines,

migrating tribes often stirred up skirmishes in the desert in order to plunder nearby farms and support themselves. Local herdsmen such as Nabal routinely accepted their presence peacefully and, in keeping with eastern hospitality, would hold a sort of open house to cement good community relations. Nabal's response to David, however, violated common gentility:

> *Who is David? ...Shall I then take my bread and my water and my meat that I have killed for my shearers, and give it to men when I do not know where they are from (1 Samuel 25:10-11)?*

David had observed a point of etiquette and been offered tactless ill breeding in return. Such behavior was unheard of! David's response was rash and thoughtless.

Put on your swords! he shouted, and with 400 of his men he moved toward reckless reprisal with Nabal's insult ringing in his ears.

Meanwhile, one of the servants rushed to Abigail with the report. David's men had come in good will but had been rebuffed. They had indeed protected the shearers in the fields but were now reacting against this rude master with a vow to kill the entire household! One of Abigail's servants reported the imminent attack, confirming David's anger and Nabal's inflammatory words: *He is such a scoundrel that one cannot speak to him.*

The servant had tossed a time-bomb to Abigail. It was probably not the first time she had heard such complaints, but this was an impossible problem. What should she do? How should she respond? The mood was ugly, but proving that her beauty was more than superficial, she demonstrated that her clear mind could unravel a complicated people problem.

Abigail's Emergency Plan

1. *Perception.* Abigail's awareness and her ability to see the situation accurately turned her in the direction of a wise solution. She knew her husband, she grasped the gravity of disrespecting the king, and she understood how to sift through various options for the best result.

2. *Action.* To strike in the presence of danger requires courage, but Abigail lost no time. She had to intervene between the anger of David and the wrath of her husband. From either direction she risked personal harm, but she acted with a charming sweetness—she resorted to her kitchen for help. Wine, meat, fresh bread and fruit were loaded quickly for the mission. She herself rode a donkey and was the first to intercept the advancing column of David's angry men.

Alighting, bowing and speaking with disarming humility, Abigail quickly quenched David's rage. She assumed blame for the entire incident but also went a step further and gently reminded David of possible consequences from his own hot-headed response. She asked forgiveness and expressed her deep concern that, as future king, he would be able to assume the throne with a clear conscience. All of this was based on a mutual allegiance to Jehovah God. They spoke the same language of faith.

3. *Honesty.* Abigail's beauty or even her intelligence would have meant little without her openness of spirit. King David recognized immediately that he had met a women who harbored no hidden agenda. No manipulation, no excuses. She faced reality as it was.

Even with her husband, there is no evidence of backlash. She simply waited until he was sober and told him what she had done. In so doing she witnessed the truth of Proverbs 5:22: *His own iniquities entrap the wicked man, and he is caught in the cords of his sin.*

Secret Ingredient

The unseen factor in Abigail's conduct lies outside the human dimension. Her experience was a slice of reality: anguish, danger and overwhelming perplexity. What she did not do is as significant as what she accomplished.

• *No self-pity*—She had every reason to try to defend herself, but this was not part of her plan.

• *No blame for Nabal*—Although she was realistic about her husband's limitations, no harsh condemnation is recorded: *He who reproves a scoffer gets shame for himself (Proverbs 9:7).*

• *No attempt at retaliation or escape*—She stayed on the job in a bad scene and continued to keep herself alert and healthy: *Vengeance is Mine, I will repay, says the Lord (Hebrews 10:30).*

Abigail followed the guiding star of God's Word. She depended on His protection, His promises and

His provision. The believer is always secure in using God's resources.

Winning Strategy

A common mistake of disgruntled wives in the twentieth century is to focus on the offending partner. God alone knows how to deal with a mate who violates the protective bond of Christian marriage. It is to Him that the injured party must look. His divine timing and His strategy often clash with human reasoning, but He alone has the real solution.

Abigail's beauty was undoubtedly an asset. Her intelligence was critical in working through a risky circumstance. Had she used her good looks and keen mind selfishly, the results would have been disastrous. Instead she walked with the grace of one who was not leaning on her own understanding. Everything about Abigail speaks of nobility. Robert D. Foster wrote:

> Abigail was a bird of rarest plumage who also had the power of music. Although her cage was dark and dirty, she had a song in the night. The name Abigail means "Cause of Joy." She didn't hit a sour note in this entire dramatic performance.[14]

History records Nabal's sudden death shortly following this episode. David then asked Abigail to become his queen.

Of all human sensations, perhaps beauty is most difficult to define. It seems elusive, ephemeral, so subjective that trying to describe it to someone else invites frustration. The poet Percy Shelley asked, "Where is the love, beauty and truth we seek in our mind?" *(Julian and Meddalo, 1819, Line 170)*

Confucius commented that "everything has its beauty but not everyone sees it," but the biblical definition of beauty ascribes its origin to the Creator. *He has made everything beautiful in its time (Ecclesiastes 3:11).* In a women's life, beauty shines through restraint; gentle and quiet spirit, an echo of Isaiah's words, *How beautiful upon the mountains are the feet of him who brings good news, who proclaims peace, who brings glad tidings of good things, who proclaims salvation, who says to Zion, Your God reigns (Isaiah 52:7)!*

The Investigator

〜

$\mathcal{N}$ellie wandered through childhood like a piece of human flotsam. Her mother had been a barmaid, taking her little girl from town to town, wherever she could get hired to mix and pour drinks. As a teen, Nellie was propelled into the same stream of rootless, immoral living in a struggle to survive and wound up on a barstool in Florida.

"Ah-m lookin' fer the mos' rotten, low-down wicked woman ah c'n find—d'yew where I c'n find one?" mumbled a bleary-eyed man beside her. Shifting from her own shell of misery, Nellie replied, "You're a-lookin' right at 'er. You won't fine nobody worse'n me!"

One year later a bright, alert Nellie told me the story of how she and her drinking buddy, who is now her husband, had both reached the bottom. Neither of them had any money, family or resources of any kind, and they ended up on a strange doorstep begging for something to eat. The only thing they had in common was heartache. He was a race-car driver. His previous up-and-down marriage had crashed. His last spark of self-respect flickered when his wife ran off with another driver—a man of criminal record and evil reputation. In his anger and humiliation, he determined to drown himself in degradation.

Nellie represents innumerable young women who desperately want to know what else can be found to loosen the choke-hold on their lives. Where can I go, what can I learn, who can help me?

When Nellie and her companion knocked on that unfamiliar door, little did they know that a hand would reach out, not only to their hungry bodies but to their starved souls as well. A loving couple took them in, sheltered them, nurtured them and introduced them to the Bread of Life.

The worst this world can offer is no match for God's ability to restore and mend a broken life. It has always been so. Ruth, the hopeless heathen maiden, found in her friend and mentor, Naomi, the outlet to hope and a future even though they also met what our world would call "rotten luck."

The Grass Is Always Greener...

Naomi and her husband, Elimilech, were moving, leaving their home town of Bethlehem, the agricultural center that later earned fame as the birthplace of Jesus Christ. Could this possibly be the Promised Land? Jehovah had vowed to bring His people here into a land of wheat and barley, of olive oil and honey, as Moses himself had said, ...*a land where you shall eat food without scarcity...(Deuteronomy 8:9, KJV).*

Elimilech (*God is king*) must have harbored strong doubts about his heritage. Parched barley fields surrounded him; dry creek-beds mocked his faith. The Promised Land, scene of highest hopes and heady victories for General Joshua, was now a near-wasteland. Bethlehem, the granary of the nation, was a weary outpost of survival. In a state of decay, the shriveled heirs of promise were scattered and discouraged and *every man did that which was right in his own eyes (Judges 21:25).* The land was ruled by inept judges and many of Elimilech's neighbors had turned to erotic Baal worship.

What were Naomi's hopes and fears as she loaded pack animals with her husband and their two young sons, closed up the house, and set out? Like many others before and since, they wanted to make a new start. Naomi and her family joined the trickle of refugees moving eastward, around the Dead Sea into the lush hills of Moab. Plentiful rains there fed the Arnon River and people prospered. But alien territory loomed ahead. Here Eglon, Moab's ruler, had in former years allied himself with local Bedouins and marched boldly into Benjamite territory, only to lose his life along with ten thousand of his men in the attempt. It was in this region where the Israelite judge Jepthah had haggled with the Ammonites on the north bank of the Arnon.

Would the people befriend a family from Judah? I suspect that personal survival overcame Elimilech's apprehension, as well as his religious convictions. He had had it with Judah and was willing to make concessions in order to find a productive farm.

It's just temporary, Elimilech and Naomi must have told each other. Israelites rarely forsook their land. Certainly they intended to return after the famine passed and the boys—Mahlon (*weak*) and Chilion (*wasting*)—had regained their strength. Here where sheep grazed on high green meadows the arable fields showed promise for a new start in life.

Disillusionment

To Naomi it was a fresh release from the choking dust of Canaan. It was a chance to answer her nagging doubt, *is bare existence all there is?* Even the sweaty toil of cultivating fields held the hope of harvest. Surely here the children would become robust.

Although the famine was behind them, Naomi and Elimilech faced a new shortage—a spiritual drought. Their neighbors blatantly worshiped idols; even the corrupt Baalism cropping up at home could not have horrified them as much as the murderous pagan rites here. You can almost see the four of them offering their lambs on a simple altar, as Moses had commanded. For this family there could be no idolatry. Their neighbors, undoubtedly, looked on with interest at these strange newcomers.

Light shines brightest in the darkness. This Israelite home must have been a focal point of interest in the community. But the family had not been settled long before death snatched away Elimilech. With desolate hearts the young men and their mother buried him in that strange land. To be away, far away, from the family and the priest at this crucial time surely added to their grief, but Naomi picked up the broken strands of her life and led her home faithfully in worshipping Jehovah.

Moabite Marriages

As Mahlon and Chilion grew into manhood, they took wives. Ruth was probably first, the wife of Mahlon, then Orpah, bride of Chilion. Two women born outside the circle of God's promises were now drawn into the warmth of a home where Jehovah, that great and terrible God who had delivered the Israelite nation out of Egypt, was believed and obeyed. Levitical law did not prohibit such marriages. Orthodox relatives would have frowned, but legally only heathen males were barred from the congregation.

For Ruth and Orpah this home stood apart from other dwellings. Honesty, purity and mutual respect of parents and children—these hallmarks of the Hebrew home beckoned to them and generated a belief in Jehovah when they were invited to become a legal part of Elimilech's family.

Nothing speaks more eloquently to a stranger than warm, loving acceptance. I vividly remember moving to Fort Worth, Texas, as a new pastor's wife. My eastern city roots were still showing in speech, attitudes and a secret disdain for this slow, homespun mentality.

Soon I learned, however, that I was the unsophisticated one. My frantic and often superficial pace of living was like a spinning wheel wildly gyrating without yarn. My snap judgments were no match for the sane, prudent decisions that brought these people not only more prosperity than I had ever seen, but a certain joie de vivre that was delightfully contagious. These marvelously magnetic strangers knew how to live. Moreover they accepted me, loved me and converted me into a contented Texan!

Ruth and Orpah certainly basked in Naomi's glow. They were accepted and loved by their husbands and their mother-in-law. Like an uninvited intruder, death hovered over the home. What a crushing blow, when their means of livelihood faded! Elimilech was gone, but Naomi nurtured and clung to her two sons, both apparently in poor health. But all her nursing knowledge, the wholesome food, the fresh air and the motherly devotion were futile against the brutal monster of disease. Ten years after leaving Bethlehem-Judah, Naomi was not only a grieving widow, but a mother without sons.

Three deaths in a family once so full of hope for the future reduced Naomi to a position of poverty and destitution. For the second time in her life all means of support seemed to be gone. Before there had been love and warmth of family. Now she was alone. Ruth and Orpah were fine young women, but what could they do?

Courage in the Clutch

Some people seem to hang on in the middle of a collapsed life. Others are flung, fragmented, into destruction. Our world has all but accepted discordant and disintegrated families. In our great love affair with what one writer has called the electronic dazzle, television teaches viewers to laugh while young people are yanked from traditional moorings and thrust into disastrous relationships. In a pattern that isolates as it connects,

> the electronic media have undoubtedly contributed to the general crisis of authority in Western societies....Media analyst Conrad Lodziak attributes to the rise of television the decline of the family as the major socializing agent...undermining the authority of the father and the protective will of the mother, resulting in social fragmentation...[15]

Have you ever talked with someone who is alone and hurting badly? What happens in the office when the salesman who was always such fun stops at your desk with a dejected look?

"What's the matter?" you ask.

"Listen, I've got to tell somebody," he whispers. "I'm in trouble—my marriage is coming unglued. I...I really don't know what to do—I've always thought of you as a friend."

"Oh, gee, I'm sorry—I really am. Maybe you ought to go see a counselor—you know, somebody who knows about those things..." You find yourself rambling, trying to say "Don't stop here—I don't have any answers!" You try to send him on with a smile, telling him not to let it get him down. You remind him he has lots of company these days.

"Yeah, well...ah...thanks. I really didn't mean to bother you." He flicks his cigarette ashes and moves away. He's reading your mind—you've tossed him in with all the other losers. He walks away, wishing his nightmare would be over. But it isn't.

Too bad, we say. But a moment's regret is the most we often give. We want to forgive and forget. We want to get back to our own lives. No time to get involved, really. I think Naomi must have sensed this dissociation from disaster as her neighbors turned away.

The tragedy forced difficult decisions. The brides had possibly severed relations with their own heathen families, having stepped into Jehovah worship. A return to their Moabite families would mean not only criticism and a return to lower status, but also likely another marriage, totally heathen.

Naomi herself had nothing to offer. The loss of any one of her men would have been calamitous, but losing all three left her with indescribable anguish and loss. Certainly there was no visible income.

Moving Out

Like wreckage floating from a devastating storm, the widows apparently buried their dead, closed their home, and approached the readied moment of separation. Naomi insisted the young women return to their mothers' homes. Was it out of love or desperation? Since Naomi experienced a sense of helplessness, she expected each of them to feel the same. Where else but to go back home?

The suggestion had merit, for oriental cultures held no status for women, but did provide women's quarters. There, presided over by a senior woman, they were given minimal protection and opportunity for marriage and motherhood.

I have come to believe that one reason God brings tragedy and overwhelming problems into our lives is to force us to exercise abilities we have never used. My mother, for example, emerged from Dad's death a different woman. His excruciating ten months of final illness left all of us exhausted, watching our virile, active, working-man, husband-father atrophy into a pain-wracked cancer victim.

Having spent every available dollar in a vain attempt to save his life, she was forced to say good-bye and bury him. In need of surgery herself, she lay totally spent in a hospital bed praying that the Lord would take her also. The future was bleak and visible resources were non-existent.

Instead God pointed her to Himself. He restored her health, gave her training and a job she never dreamed possible. He can and does make the lame to walk again.

But those who wait on the Lord shall renew their strength; they shall mount up with wings like eagles, they shall run and not be weary, they shall walk and not faint (Isaiah 40:31).

Naomi proved that God never forsakes those who trust Him. Although bitter in spirit, her motives were just and her method was to do what was right for each of her daughters. She herself had to return to Judah, finding her way, as wounded animals do in the woods, to the place where she was born.

Split Decision

Orpah's decision to return to her mother's home was sound. She would lose honor and position, but bereavement had come at any early age and she was an eligible wife. Ruth, whose name means "a friend," could not be persuaded to go. Refusing to bow to the circumstance, she responded instead to Naomi's strength. Her reply is poignant poetry:

Do not urge me to leave you or turn back from following you; for where you go, I will go, and where you lodge, I will lodge. Your people shall be my people, and your God, my God. Where you die, I will die, and there I will be buried (Ruth 1:16-17, NASB).

Although her fidelity must have warmed Naomi's heart, did it also breed uncertainty? Did she really want responsibility for this young life? She welcomed the companionship, but bringing home an immigrant was risky.

Still the force of Ruth's decision lay in her fierce drive to gain what Naomi had. She had thought through the implication of leaving her homeland. She had cast her vote not so much with this individual whom she had come to love and respect, but with Naomi's God, His people and the land He gave them. She sensed an eternal dimension to Naomi's faith that transcended even her deepest heartaches. It was a tie to the supernatural, the decoding of her lifelong riddle. Clearly God Himself had changed Ruth's heart; she had become a true believer.

Although she had never seen it, the land of Canaan

drew Ruth like a magnet. Not only the birthplace of the ones she loved, it was also the source of this life-changing faith that stood in stark contrast to all her heathen background. She willingly gave up her name, her citizenship, her very identity to become a prose-lyte Jewess. Her conversion was complete and gen-uine because of this woman Naomi.

The columnist Carl Rowan wrote a tribute to his mother-in-law, who had died at age ninety. Having been reared in slave country, she married a humble man but retained lifelong pride and self esteem.

> I would give a week of salary every month to anyone with a successful formula for creating throughout black America the sense of family, the quest for achievement, the respect for learning, the motivation of children...that his parents-in-law produced.[16]

It was a similar flame that burned inside Naomi and ignited Ruth.

The tender tale of Ruth and Naomi portrays our womanly will to patrol the perilous frontiers of our lives. Graciously God hovers over us, always ready to hear our "Mayday" calls. Blaise Pascal, the seventeenth-century genius of faith, wrote:

> We have to know when to doubt, when to affirm what is certain, and when to submit. Anyone who acts otherwise does not understand the force of reason.[17]

The Caregiver

*L*ike a giant searchlight the voice of God found Eve huddling with her husband, hiding from her Creator and no doubt hating herself for capitulating to the words of a lowly serpent. How terrifying must have been those moments in confrontation! How humiliating to admit that she had dared to disbelieve, distrust and detach herself from the pleasant and orderly contentment of her garden home.

Did Eve cower in dread that the Almighty would take away her honored appointment as the one to bear Adam's children? He had commanded the couple to be fruitful and multiply; had she ruined that prospect? No, but He spoke about "pain." The root of that word means "injury." Children would indeed be hers to conceive and to deliver into the world, but with great difficulty and deep grief. The word for "pains" or "heaviness" was repeated when the Lord spoke to Adam about the fruit of the field: *Through painful toil you shall eat of it all the days of your life (Genesis 3:17, NIV).*

The noted German theological scholar F. Delitzsch wrote:

> That the woman should bear children was the original will of God; but it was a punishment that henceforth she was to bear them in sorrow; i.e., with pains which threatened her own life as well as that of the child.[18]

Weakened by sin, her joyful anticipation of child-birth was clouded, but it was also a means of subduing the serpent. God said that her seed would crush his head. One after another the Old Testament narratives step across the centuries to record that reality. Hannah sparkles as a noble woman. It was rather an inelegant meeting between a would-be mother and a profes-sional priest when the beginnings of her very note-worthy son were decided.

Application for Motherhood

Hannah and her husband, Elkanah, lived during a sordid mixture of politics and religion that seesawed in the central highlands of Palestine a thousand years before Christ. He was a Levite of priestly heritage living in the tribe of Ephraim, among the hills piled up between the Great Sea and the Jordan River. No land had been assigned to the tribe of Levi; they were scattered in specified cities.

Early Israel apparently practiced very little polygamy, but Hannah was caught in a three-sided marriage, a domestic triangle. Although she was loved by her husband, she was despised by the other wife. Only Jacob and Gideon up to this point in the Bible are reported as giving full wifehood status to more than one woman at a time. Elkanah had two wives. Probably Hannah's infertility occasioned the second marriage to Peninnah, who bore him children. Jewish survival demanded a high birth rate to create a strong, growing nation.

Today's western women regard polygamy as simply a title in a sociology text, but the wife who must live with other wives knows cheerlessness and disillusionment. My memory stirs to a rude shock of reality that occurred when I visited Nigeria in 1974.

Several days after I addressed a short series of women's meetings in Jos, a committee called on me to present a gift and have tea. I am still moved as I reflect on the generosity of those dear women, who were economically deprived but full of a giving spirit. Physically lean and muscular, weathered with hard work in and out of doors, the glow of Christ's peace and love softened their weary faces.

Through an interpreter we discussed the meetings and then one of the leaders asked if she might present a prayer request. She came near to tears as she described her marital problem. Her husband, a professing Christian, had announced he was taking another wife into the family.

Although the other women registered immediate shock, I was too naive to comprehend the impact. Through the language barrier she explained that a new wife would bring her humiliation and demotion.

She, and especially her children, would suffer discrimination. She would get less to eat and more work to do. Already her life was almost unbearable. How, she asked me, could Christ allow this to happen?

This was one of many times in my life when I had no answer. I simply bowed my head and said in my heart, "Oh, God, there, but for your grace, I would be." We prayed together and I felt like a kindergartner with graduate students in the college of experience. We laid it before God and thanked Him that He always leads us to triumph in Christ (2 Corinthians 2:14).

Family Frustration

Peninnah taunted Hannah because of her barrenness. The writer of 1 Samuel says she "provoked her relentlessly." I remember a fitting description: *Her faults were little faults and the scars accumulated like X-ray burns.* It was not enough that Hannah suffered the unspoken disgrace of having no children; she also endured a constant shower of petty criticism. But there is no evidence that Hannah ever retorted. She must have ached inside, but God often permits irritations to reveal His sufficiency. He is able to keep us going under the worst conditions.

A devout believer in Jehovah, Elkanah shepherded his family annually over the twelve-mile trip to worship at Shiloh, where they offered sacrifices according to the Holy Law. There the family worshiped Jehovah Sabaoth, the Lord of Hosts. How pointless that must have seemed when their nation was weak politically and the hostile Philistines periodically flexed their military muscles along the borders. Canaanite idolatry was practiced increasingly by the Israelites and the priesthood was nearly powerless.

Hannah wanted a son. For years it had been so, but now her desire was uncontrollable and her sadness spilled over into weeping. Elkanah, a loving, concerned husband, tried to comfort his gentle-spirited wife. It was a difficult situation but he was not driven to desperation. Hannah, on the other hand, was at the breaking point. She had a two-fold problem: personal and national. Both looked hopeless. The problem had mounted up and overwhelmed her.

Elkanah applied masculine logic. He asked four questions: *Why are you crying? Why are you not eating? Why is your heart grieved? Am I not better to you than ten sons?*

Remember that this husband made no secret of the fact that he loved Hannah. With such emotional support, why would she cry? He had served her, the record states, a worthy portion; that is, the choicest of food. With that in front of her, why couldn't she eat? Of course there was the matter of no children, but he had tried to make it up to her. Why couldn't she accept reality?

Hannah's desolation was peculiarly a woman's problem. How could a husband know the emptiness she felt in being denied the privilege of giving birth? How could he experience a loss of appetite over her empty nest? Did he share her fear for her people, God's chosen nation? Did he possess the sensitive insight to discern the immoral thoughts of the young priests as they went about their duties in the temple? Was he torn with terror over the obvious decay of their center of worship?

Prescription for Prayer

Hannah had a plan. To put it into action she left her plate untouched and made her way to the post of the temple. This was not Solomon's temple of generations later, but it was the place of worship established by Joshua when the nation of Israel took possession of the land. There Hannah prayed and wept. Many women do that, but she did one thing more. She made a vow. It could be said that up to this point her desire for a son was merely selfish and defensive, an effort to meet the competition under her own roof. Now her motive was altered; she exercised her will to ask for a son, not for herself but for the Lord God.

God's people have always struggled with this matter of talking to Him in prayer. Many feel there must be a key, certain words that unlock the Almighty's door. Why is it that some people seem to get answers and others pray in vain?

There is a key to prayer. It shows up in the prayers of the Bible, especially in the Old Testament. They are based on pleas to God to keep His promises. He will always do that. This fact accounts for the many times the phrases "for Thy name's sake" and "according to Thy word" are used. In the New Testament Peter says, *The Lord is not slow about His promise (2 Peter 3:9, NIV)*. These prayers God delights to answer, but He does not indulge selfish whims.

I know this truth from personal experience. I once prayed for a house for the wrong reasons. Finally I came to the point where I could say, "All right, Lord, if you want me to live here my whole life, I'm willing. I pray only for the grace to do it." It was then that the Lord moved with amazing speed to change my situation. I knew unmistakably that my new home was His gift. It belonged to Him and was to be used for Him.

Hannah's decision to give her son back to God could not have been a spur-of-the-moment act of contrition. Otherwise, she would surely have backed down when she found herself holding that long-awaited baby boy in her arms. Unquestionably she had debated with herself and probed her own desires: Why do you want this son?

It is not difficult to see why Elkanah loved her. She was perceptive, courageous and totally honest. She possessed a mother's heart. Most importantly, she was full of faith, a reminder that *without faith it is impossible to please God, because anyone who comes to Him must believe that He exists, and that He rewards those who earnestly seek Him (Hebrews 11:6, NIV).* What a legacy to leave to her boy, a man whom God listed among the heroes of faith centuries later.

Hannah was hemmed in. We have all been there with her. Totally frustrated, unable to move. No exit. A dead end. Let me cite a simple illustration.

Suppose I need to go somewhere. I am under pressure, but I cannot get my car out of the garage. I have the car, the fuel, the license and the know-how to

drive but I remain boxed in. The door is shut. I can push and pull, even try to kick it open, but my little bit of strength and strategy against the big door is ridiculously mismatched. However, I have one bit of knowledge; this door that blocks my way between imprisonment and freedom is responsive to a higher source of power—electricity. Not just any application of electricity, but a formula, a wavelength worked out for my individual garage door. I press the button; the door opens. I am free.

It happens often. We are hopelessly tied down by forces far beyond our moving. Yet deeply implanted in our heart is a release button. We have access to the power of all the universe. *Let us then approach the throne of grace with confidence, so that we may receive mercy and find grace to help us in our time of need (Hebrews 4:16, NIV).*

Hannah prayed for a son with the holy intent of giving him as a living sacrifice to God. It is doubtful that she had any grandiose plan to save her nation. Like Mary breaking the alabaster box of ointment upon Christ, she "did what she could." God honored that step of faith.

God's Nod of Approval

The decline of the clergy seems to stand out in the failure of the old priest Eli to recognize Hannah's true penitence. He mistook supplication for insobriety. It should be noted that prayer was usually offered audibly, but it was consonant with Hannah's nature not to verbalize this personal, intimate matter.

Even as she held her tongue in anger and frustration with Peninnah, so she barely whispered her agony and hopes to Jehovah.

This praying woman had a concern that was national, but her immediate goal was personal. It involved God as the prime mover and herself as His tool. Whatever the problem, the source of power must be adequate to solve it and the means of solving it must be available.

Eli the priest responded to this weeping, incoherent supplicant with a blessing, but the very fact that he suspected drunkenness reveals the low level of personal piety among the people. Nevertheless, God gave Hannah peace of heart. She left with her burden lifted. Her contract was made with the Lord, not the priest.

A Thankful Mother

After the birth of Samuel, Hannah prayed a prayer of thanksgiving that reveals her thinking. God sees everything, she announced. *For the Lord is a God of knowledge and with Him actions are weighed (1 Samuel 2:3, NIV).* Her positive confidence in God is in sharp contrast to her sadness before she turned her problem over to Him. Transfused with joy, she sketched a bold outline of God's holiness, His power and His unchanging nature. Like a warrior charging into battle, she lashed at the proud, greedy and wicked enemies of Israel who will be the objects of Jehovah's judgment. Her words are reminiscent of the writing on the wall at the feast of Belshazzar hundreds of years later: *You have been*

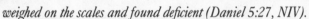

weighed on the scales and found deficient (Daniel 5:27, NIV).

This imagery of the balance scale was often used in ancient cultures. The Egyptian *Book of The Dead*, for example, recorded that the heart of a deceased person is weighed on the scale against the symbol of Truth and Right before he is admitted to the Realm of Isiris.

The place of Hebrew women in these early days is also noteworthy. This narrative shows Hannah to be her own person. In conversations with her husband and with the priest, she was treated as an equal. Later, when the child was born, the decision of when to go to Shiloh was entirely Hannah's. Even naming of the baby seems to have been influenced by his mother.

Elkanah acted with tender respect and loving protection. As a wife, Hannah most certainly bowed to her husband's wishes, but there was obviously a mutual esteem. Do what seems best to you. *Stay here until you have weaned (1 Samuel 1:23, NIV).* Elkanah's response to his wife shows high regard for her and for their son, and for his confidence in God's future guidance.

Keeping the baby Samuel at home until he was weaned would traditionally mean several years, possibly four or five. Elkanah readily agreed with the decision to allow Samuel to remain at home with his mother until that time. Then, faithful to their word, the parents appeared together before Eli, bringing the animal sacrifice along when the child was presented. *So now I give him to the Lord. For his whole life he will be given over to the Lord (1 Samuel 1:28, NIV).*

These are Hannah's words, fully legal and accepted in this patriarchal society.

The intensity of Hannah's faith glows from the page as she places this young, impressionable boy in the hands of Eli, a man she knew to be an unworthy and incapable father. There was no hesitation; she and God understood each other. This was the moment of truth for Hannah.

Henry Ward Beecher once said that a mother's heart is the child's schoolroom. During those first formative years Samuel undoubtedly learned his spiritual ABC's from his godly mother. Modern researchers tell us a child's emotional framework is formed by the time he is three years old. Israel's future leader was well prepared by his mother.

Rewards of Keeping a Vow

When Hannah left young Samuel in the temple, she sang aloud an outburst of praise, the overflow of a liberated heart. As surely as the dawn follows the darkness, God gives joy and freedom to those who give their best to Him.

Returning home with her husband, mother Hannah began the routine of loving her little son at a distance. Any mother can attest to the strain, the questions: *Does he miss me? Will he manage all right by himself? Will he get homesick? Will he eat as he should? Will he stay covered when he is asleep?* One can only imagine the number of times she talked to God about her boy.

Every year there was mounting eagerness as the time came to visit Shiloh. Anticipation? Yes, but perhaps also a trace of anxiety. Surely Hannah knew, as all who worshipped at the temple must have known, that Eli's sons were wicked men. They seduced the women worshipers and feasted on the food given for sacrifice. What sort of influence would they have on the impressionable little Samuel?

Such matters would be resolved by God. Hannah had her agreement with Him. She was now bearing other children and preparing each year for the return visit to the temple. Her maternal love is poignantly recorded: *Each year his mother made him a little robe and took it to him when she went up with her husband to offer the annual sacrifice (1 Samuel 2:19, NIV).* This robe was one of distinction, commonly worn by kings, prophets and other people of position and rank. With this handmade symbol of her faith, it was evident that she saw her son as an honored servant of Jehovah.

Whenever a child of God stretches himself out in total belief, he is rewarded many times over. Having given Samuel entirely and irrevocably to the Lord, Hannah was given five additional children. He is a rewarder of those who seek him.

Hannah exemplifies the maternal heart, but what of those many women who cannot or do not wish to have children? What about those whose little ones are snatched away or whose children reject or disown their mother? As Eve taught us from her early desolation, any deviation from God's holy purpose exacts a distressful toll. Our nurturing nature fits us for the task of preparing the next generation, whether or not they are our own birth children.

That same ability draws us to anyone in need of a caring touch, a soft word of encouragement, a motherly word of advice—or a prolonged dedication to some need. For a disquieted world God wielded an effective weapon against loneliness and despair with His inquisitive, practical and tender idea of women, His natural nursemaids. How great is our mandate to display God's gift of mothering!

The Controller

On that overcast day in the garden when the eyes of God looked in sadness on the fallen woman, the loving Creator was forced by Eve's disobedience to remove her from the danger zone into which she had stepped. Before her sin she was protected by her husband, totally surrounded by love in a world that operated to perfection. Now she was estranged from her Maker; she had rebelled against His holy command. Undoubtedly her husband was angry with her; still she needed his protection.

According to the New Testament (1 Timothy 2:14) Adam was not deceived. He understood the principles of obedience and of human responsibility. Moreover, he loved Eve and he wanted her. She was his counterpart, his complement. He needed her. Therefore, God explicitly stated that although her desire (that is, her yearnings) would be for Adam, he would rule over her. The thought connotes a desire for control. It hints of feminine wiles and exploitation. In the long run, however, man would dominate her life.

Just as Sarah portrayed the quality of management, so her daughter-in-law, Rebekah, modeled the fine art of womanly manipulation. Sarah bore a son, Isaac, in her old age; and he grieved deeply when his mother died. He was comforted when his father's servant brought the beautiful Rebekah to be his bride (Genesis 24:67). But she, like Sarah, was also barren; Isaac prayed for her and the Lord helped her to conceive.

Take-Charge Tendency

The pregnancy was an unusual one. Rebekah felt jostling in her womb and wondered why, so she inquired of the Lord and His answer came to her:

Two nations are in your womb, and two peoples from within you will be separated; one people will be stronger than the other, and the older will serve the younger (Genesis 25:23, NIV).

The twins, Esau and Jacob, were opposites. Esau, the first-born, was a skilled hunter, an outdoorsman with a ruddy complexion and hairy skin. Jacob quietly stayed at home and apparently became a mama's boy. When Isaac grew old and his eyesight dimmed, he came to the important time of bestowing the family birthright on his elder son.

But he did not know that an altercation had occurred between his boys. Coming home very hungry one day, Esau smelled stew that was cooking and asked his brother for some of it. The cunning and envious Jacob jumped at a chance to cop the coveted prize. He offered to sell the stew for Esau's birthright. At that moment Esau cared nothing for the rights and privileges of the blessing and agreed to the deal.

Isaac, sensing that he would soon die, called Esau as the elder son with a request that he go shoot some game and prepare his favorite dish to celebrate the occasion of bestowing the birthright. Rebekah overheard the proposal and acted quickly to subvert her husband's plan. She wanted Jacob to have the birthright and she remembered the prophecy about the babies. Her plan of deceit called for Jacob to bring her two goats to prepare Isaac's favorite food, to dress him in Esau's clothing and to cover his smooth skin with goat's hair.

Jacob joined her in the diabolical plan, lying to his father and pretending to be his older brother. The goat hair belied his identity as Isaac identified him by smell and proceeded to pronounce the blessing. Hardly had he left when Esau came in and identified himself. With high emotions the father and son realized the trickery. But it could not be undone. When Esau begged for a blessing of some kind, Isaac spoke a prophecy that Esau would indeed serve his younger brother and that he would live by the sword.

Long-term hostility fractured the family. Jacob left home and Rebekah never saw him again. Her underhanded scheme illustrates well the damage of a woman who misuses her influence. She preempted her husband's decision-making and brought sorrow and regret to herself and her entire family.

Rebekah opens the door to the inscrutable

mystique of the female mind. She combines the maddening contradiction of physical beauty and shrewd evasion. She is the nursery rhyme girl who, when she was good was very, very good, but when she was bad she was horrid. Her favorite son, Jacob, inherited from her a life of hardship, but the eternal purpose of the Creator continued. Although Rebekah used the unique relationship of husband and wife for her own ends, Jehovah God in His grace accomplished His all-wise purposes.

Leadership and Teamwork

History records no end of tales about the duplicity and subterfuge hidden in the feminine mindset. The same woman who willingly disobeyed God in the garden lives on in the resolute determination of us, her daughters, to finagle and frustrate as we see fit.

We can also act constructively. It is the same strength of purpose that kept American women pushing forward to settle the West. They were shapers of the family, the internal dynamic of the household. One of every five was pregnant en route. Many were widowed because of frequent accidents, but, "no woman ever placed her wagon and her family under the protection of another family...women were more independent—and independent in more ways—than has been commonly assumed."[19]

We women have limitless opportunity for good or for evil with our natural take-charge drive. But leadership that builds demands a servant spirit and a willingness to work with and for others. What will be our legacy?

Part Three

WHY IS SHE IMPORTANT?

THE JEWEL
If a woman understands who she is in divine perspective, she can move herself into her rightful position of royalty by allowing God to take charge of her life.

THE MANAGER
Putting her own life in order is a natural womanly inclination, but for success she must follow Biblical guidelines for jumping the hurdles.

THE BEAUTICIAN
Her preference for prettiness will be crushed unless a woman allows the Lord Himself to open her eyes to see His version of beauty.

THE INVESTIGATOR
Dead-ends abound in our world's system, but God's promise of His Spirit to teach a woman about life makes every day an exciting prospect.

THE CAREGIVER

The womanly instinct for tending to other people with concern is ready-made for this world's ills, but only when she exercises the touch of the Master will she experience indescribable fulfillment.

THE CONTROLLER

Living as a woman in a man's world lends itself to unbearable disappointment, except that God has provided for woman His ingenious method of excelling beyond circumstances.

Getting
God's Viewpoint

∽

$\mathcal{I}$n Canada I met Swiss-born Ursula who told me this story. At the end of World War II her mother's fiancé was listed as missing in action, presumed dead. Since she was an insecure orphan, she accepted a marriage proposal from a wealthy man and bore him two daughters. She did not love him and he treated her shabbily. Eventually, however, her lover came home, ill and emaciated. After his mother nursed him back to health, he left Switzerland for a business in Vancouver, British Columbia, and asked Ursula's mother to leave the country and join him.

Accepting no money, she sought a divorce and used her last resources to finance the trip to North America by boat, then by train from Halifax. She could neither read nor write English. Each morning on the five-day cross-country train she took her two little girls to the wash room to comb and braid their hair. She always noticed a man waiting at the door with his shaving cup, but not until the end of the trip did she realize she had been using the men's wash room. Also, during the long journey Ursula and her sister and mother ate sandwiches and cold drinks from a vendor because they did not know there was a dining car.

Like that Swiss emigrant, many of us have no knowledge of who we are in God's grand design for women. Why is that important to us today? What impact does that ancient history have upon this last decade of the century? The confused women in our world today bear little resemblance to the regal role God intended, but He promises His help.

Divine Assistance

Just as the Creator called light out of darkness, and order out of chaos, so He continues to call splendor out of sadness and despair. People in His plan do not erode and disappear. Ponder this touching verse reflecting on restoration from the Old Testament prophet Hosea:

> *God understands your heart as well. He speaks to you today:*
>
> *I formed your body long before you knew what life would hold.*
>
> *I stood by waiting patiently for you to turn to me in love.*
>
> *I waited while you turned your back instead to taste life's "greater pleasures."*

I watched while sin's chains bound you to the auction block.

And then I paid the price to buy you back—though you were rightly mine.

I've loved you with an everlasting love,

With gentle lovingkindness drawn you close.

I claimed your tarnished soul a second time.

Don't turn away again. I've called you mine.[20]

If we ignore or deny our roots of the distant past— or the One who planted them—then all our tomorrows are mortally wounded.

When the woman sinned she hurt herself and found herself estranged from God, but she did not derail the divine purpose. God went right on using women who would believe Him.

When the descendants of the believing couple, Abraham and Sarah, were seemingly doomed to extinction in the slave camps of Egypt, Jehovah God reached down through His prophet Moses and rescued them. He would bring them into the Promised Land, as He said. Humanly speaking, however, Moses survived the Pharaoh's infanticide only because of the stubborn courage of his mother, Jochabed (Exodus 2).

Again and again He delivered them from the hand of their oppressors. Throughout the Old Testament only a handful of women dared to pierce the strong tribal restraints and believe what God had said, in spite of circumstances. Deborah rose to lead her nation; *The Lord, the God of Israel, commands you, (Judges 4:6, NIV)* she insisted. Abigail (1 Samuel 25) dared to risk her life for a godly principle. Hannah begged God for her son, Samuel, and gave him back to become a judge and a prophet, the pivotal priest in establishing the monarchy. Because Naomi and Ruth clung to what God had said, King David would be born and anointed to serve his country as sovereign. His heirs, though pounded by a history of defection, would survive the centuries to the *fullness of time (Galatians 4:4)* when God's love would be born in the Person of His Son Jesus Christ.

The New Testament records a revolutionary turnabout when Jesus the Messiah lifted the status of women. He dealt as tenderly with the woman taken in adultery (John 8) as He did with His mother, Mary. Nothing in all of human history has protected and elevated the fortunes of women as has our Judeo-Christian heritage.

Why this dogmatism? Because God created us as His crowning jewel and, despite our self-destructive tendencies, His purposes will not be thwarted. God is our Creator; He is also our re-Creator. It is not enough to fathom the depths of history or even to comprehend what God does for some women today; we women must *taste and see that the Lord is good (Psalm 34:8).* God deals in individual lives. He is a loving, involved Heavenly Father, providing detailed, hands-on assistance.

Woman in Charge

The United States has witnessed an explosion of women-owned and women-run businesses. According to the Small Business Administration, the share of all businesses that are owned by women may rise to 38 percent by the year 2000.[21] We as women tend to gravitate to retail trade, finance and services. Not much has changed over the centuries. In her scholarly book, *Women's Work, The First 20,000 Years*,[22] Elizabeth Wayland Barber explains that women have always worked in the sectors of society where children could be watched close at hand. We have moved into areas that touch the lives of women: textiles and clothing manufacture, food and nursing services. Today dollars have spilled onto the laps of women, making financial markets an added feminine concern.

Historically the sciences have commanded a male brain-trust but that, too, has changed. Wellesley College has released a study of the forces that shape a

woman's decisions. They asked whether women pre-
ferred problems with definitive answers or ones
where multiple interpretations were possible. The
most significant single predictor of whether she
remained in science was that she like precise
answers.[23] The sciences are naturally attractive to the
vigorous, put-it-in-place, feminine brain.

God has no problem with his daughters using their
talents in commercial leadership. She may be Lydia
selling her brilliant and expensive fabrics (Acts 16:14)
or the Warsaw-born Madame Marie Sklodowska
Curie winning Nobel Prizes: 1903 in chemistry, and,
with her husband, 1911 in physics. Their daughter
Irene repeated her mother's honor in 1935. Together
the family laid much of the foundation for later
research in nuclear physics and chemistry.

Our world is waking up to the resources hidden in
the heads of women. Sally Helgesen[24] has profiled
four American women, current corporate leaders, to
explain how women manage their responsibilities.
Such qualities as long-term negotiating, listening
with an ear for inner feelings and creating ambiance
in the work place have paid off handsomely. We must
understand that the dignity accorded to women in the
workplace derives from the founding principles of our
nation based upon biblical precepts.

The ethical standards of the marketplace are rooted
in ancient codes. The code of Hammurabi, for example,
called for fair play and honesty in weights and measure, authenticity in services and goods traded and a
trust relationship between businessmen. It called for

fair treatment of women, but they were not considered anything more than valuable property to be carefully kept.

The law from Sinai, The Ten Commandments, struck the radical note of honoring father *and* mother, equating the two. It was the wisdom of the Proverbs which warned men against foolish, adulterous women and strongly advised young men to *not forsake your mother's teaching.*

Throughout the wisdom literature of the Bible (Job through Song of Solomon) the wise woman is promoted. I call the portrait of the woman in Proverbs 31 "A Woman For All Seasons." She is totally feminine, but this paragon of a wife clearly delineates daily priorities. First is her husband. *The heart of her husband safely trusts her.* Unheard of in the ancient world! She does not manipulate him: *she will do him good and not evil all the days of her life (Proverbs 31:11,12, KJV).* Many women have told me they come away from this chapter tired, out of breath. It jumps up and grabs us! We can't help but notice the food she prepares, the way she cares for herself and others. I remember Sam Levinson's quip, *We had a permissive father; he permitted us to work.*[25]

> Calm and efficient, capable and quick
> She never makes me feel I should be, too—
> She cultivated long ago the trick
> Of doing all the things she had to do
> Without a lot of fuss. I never feel
> Reproved, rebuffed, or put the least bit down
> If sometimes fumbling—for she never deals

In sarcasm, or frowns a wary frown.
There is a motive underlying this:
A choice she must have made from early on
To overlook whatever seems amiss;
To recognize the good and then be gone.
Her competence is so adorned with grace
She leaves a benediction in each place.[26]

Work defines a woman's world, whether or not she is employed outside of her home. How she does it reflects her womanliness, but it also betrays her inner convictions. Notice that every woman is profiled in the Bible to reveal her heart attitude, for this is what God considers to be of crucial importance. We are left with searching questions: do we imitate our Creator who worked for six days making this magnificent earth? Do we allow our God-given beauty to shine through our tasks? If so, we earn His favor and we gain respect and status. *Give her of the fruit of her hands, and let her own works praise her in the gates* (Proverbs 31:31).

Beauty Is Not for Sale

Lisa surfaced in my life at a youth leaders' conference. She did not fit the stereotype of the extrovertish phys-ed teacher. But she was a standout, a smashing blonde with big brown eyes exuding poise and careful grooming. I found that Lisa was born into a wealthy home, the only child of parents who were themselves only children from genteel backgrounds. Lisa had everything this world could offer, but something seemed amiss for her, so she began attending a Bible study where she made a profession of faith in Christ.

At the last meeting before a summer break the leader told them that, since they had been taking in so much, it was time to get involved with giving out. Lisa reflected that there was nothing she could do or wanted to do, but then, she told me, some "weirdo" said to her, "Hey, I'm on the God squad at Juvenile Hall, wanna come?"

Her decision to go with him was solely because she could then say that she had truly been to "the other side of the tracks." In her words, "When I got there, it was strange. I could feel myself being drawn into it, kind of wonderful. Imagine, 200 kids, two-thirds boys, and they all needed somebody. Somehow I knew what they were feeling; they had never been loved, and I had found real love in Jesus Christ. Suddenly I knew I *had* to tell them!"

Lisa is now a regular staff member, specializing in sixteen-to-eighteen-year-olds. Her soft beauty is a tool God is using to turn young lives toward Himself. But it would have been wasted, had she not volunteered herself for His assignment.

Beauty is the synchronizing of our senses. It can be described with words, but that is only the packaging. The real essence is felt deeply inside our beings. Perhaps that is why music changes behavior; the soothing of a lullaby or the spurring into battle of the marching band. Singing punctuates the Old Testament record because God's people organized their worship around lavish vocal and instrumental praise to their Creator. Heaven will hear not only the song of Moses but also a new song of adoration to the Lamb who was slain.

True beauty always heals, unites, restores and perfects that which it touches. Therefore it must be intrinsic; only the originator, God Himself, can create that. We make a stab at decorating or glamorizing, but only the outside changes. No wonder Peter advises wives, *Your beauty should not come from outward adornment...Instead it should be that of your inner self, the unfading beauty of a gentle and quiet spirit, which is of great worth in God's sight (1 Peter 3:3-4, NIV).*

Touched by Real Beauty

God's most poignant exclamation of beauty came at the manger of Bethlehem. The beauty began with a young woman in her little hovel in Nazareth. If we could peel off the scales of twenty centuries, we would see an obscure and dirty little village on a hillside. It probably would not have been there at all, except for the ancient trade route winding north toward Damascus. People there were merchants and tradesmen speaking simple, common Aramaic. Their beliefs were a corrupted Judaism. It is probably safe to say that, with very few exceptions, folks in Nazareth had given up on the great Jehovah of the law and the prophets.

Under the harsh rule of the hated Herods and the ruthless Roman legions hope was hard to come by. Mary's family was poor, but rich in things that really matter. She knew of the Messiah promised to Israel. What would He look like? What tribe? What family? And then it happened—it happened to her. *Congratulations favored lady! The Lord is with you!* From an angel the words came to her, a mere teenager.

Our celebrity-sotted world knows teens who feign humility. *Oh, no! You can't mean li'l ole me!* Young girls might jump up and down for joy as if a beauty queen had been announced. *Wow! Just think, I get to be the chosen one.* If she were a modern young girl, Mary could have just fainted away in a dramatic swoon.

Not this Mary of Nazareth. She was completely poised and emotionally stable, but she was also human. She was afraid. *Don't be frightened, Mary. God has decided to wonderfully bless you (Luke 1:28-31).* The angel proceeded to tell her that she would bear a son who would be the Savior of the world. She had to ask him the obvious question: *How would she become pregnant when she was a virgin?*

The Holy Spirit Himself would come to her and she would conceive the Son of God. But Mary was human; was this a vision, a figment of her imaginary longings? No, there was proof. Her older cousin, Elizabeth was also miraculously pregnant. The time was ripe for God to visit His people.

Immediately Mary rushed to the home of Elizabeth and her priest-husband, Zecharias, who lived in the highlands of Judea. Sure enough, Elizabeth was not only expecting a son, also promised by this same angel, Gabriel, but she greeted Mary with a glad cry, *You are favored by God above all other women...What an honor that the mother of my Lord should visit me!* For three critical months, the first trimester of her pregnancy, Mary stayed with her relatives, away from the poverty of her home, away from the ignorant criticism, and close to the priest who not only understood but legally would vouch for Mary's purity.

Going back to Nazareth had its problems. Undoubtedly Mary had been concerned about what Joseph, her fiancé, would think. Engagement in her culture was a firm promise to marry, but Mary and

Joseph had not as yet lived together. That matter had also been tended by the angel with a total explanation (Matthew 1:18-23). In obedience Joseph took Mary as his wife.

It seems that Quirinius, the Roman ruler, had ordered a census, a means of raising taxes. It meant that all families had to go to their birthplace or hometown of the tribe and register—in person. Joseph had to go to Bethlehem, more than four day's journey. It was scheduled at Mary's due date, but there was no choice. The Roman government could not care less about some Jewish girl having a baby!

No details are known until the young couple arrived at Bethlehem. Surely the trip on the back of a donkey must have been a wretched one for Mary, and the prospect of staying in the inn was deplorable. Decent people despised them. They were drafty and noisy, inhabited by rude and coarse patrons. It was evidently wintertime and there was no room at the inn, so the hapless pair was sent to the stable.

How gracious of God! In the winter, farmers put most of their cattle in caves; only the woolly sheep and goats stayed on the hills. Thus in the cave there was fresh straw and water. The animals heated it comfortably and it was cradled in a manger that the Son of God appeared to man. The grandeur of that scene cannot be adequately enlivened by words. In the heavens the angel chorus sang, *Glory to God in the highest heaven, and peace on earth for all those pleasing him (Luke 2:14, LB).*

Maximum beauty touched the earth that night. It is great art, the essence of splendor, which includes humor, pathos and pain. Much of what we see as repulsive in isolation becomes beautiful in relation. We have only to study the birth of the Baby, contemplate it and embrace it in order to comprehend the power of beauty in our world.

Inward Beauty at Work

In God's economy the apparently fragile thing becomes vigorous when it is dedicated to the honor of what is good and right. Mark Twain recalled a scene from his European youth. A frenzied man was chasing his daughter through the town with a rope. The terrified girl, looking for a refuge, slipped inside Twain's mother's front door. Instead of closing it and locking it after her, his mother stood in the doorway with her arms stretched across it.

The man swore and cursed, threatening Twain's mother with the rope. She showed no signs of fear, did not flinch, but only stood up straight and looked him in the eye. She shamed him and defied him in a voice not audible in the street, but clearly directed at the man's conscience and dormant manhood. The man handed her the rope and with a great, blasphemous oath declared that she was the bravest woman he had ever seen. They remained good friends for years. The confident poise of a beautiful woman conquered the cowardice of a weak-minded man out of control.

A Nose for Good News

❧

Epictetus, a first century emancipated slave, became a stoic philosopher who taught the people of Athens that they should behave with politeness, taking only as much from life as they needed. He is purported to have asked this question: Why do we not get angry if someone says we have a headache, yet are very angry if someone says we are arguing foolishly or illogically? The answer, of course, lies in our certainty. If there is no headache, what does it matter what he thinks? But I am startled, uneasy, if he contradicts my idea or my belief, and more so if a hundred others also disagree with me.

What is right tends to be debatable. It was not so until the serpent questioned God's words of warning; for the first time the woman saw that the fruit was *desirable for gaining wisdom*. The tempter had suggested that if she ate the fruit she would be like God, knowing good and evil. Evil, of course, was an unknown factor in her world, but she decided to go for it. What did she have to lose? Everything.

In our present society we debate values. The introduction to William J. Bennett's *The Book Of Virtues* states:

> Today we speak about values and how important it is to 'have them,' as if they were beads on a string or marbles in a pouch. But these stories speak to morality and virtues not as something to be possessed, but as the central part of human nature, not as something to have but as something to be, the most important thing to be.[27]

What we are, of course, is the nub of all our strivings for finding out more. The thirst for knowledge is slaked by the confidence that comes from feeling we are superior to others. Therein lies power.

The seventeenth-century thinker, Blaise Pascal, jolts our contemporary conclusions with this comment:

> ...it is right to follow the right, but it is necessary to follow the powerful: Right without might is helpless, whereas might without right is tyrannical. Right without might is challenged because there are always unjust people around. Power without justice is to be condemned. Justice and power must therefore be combined so that we can ensure that what is right is strong, or that what is strong is just.[28]

As a woman with Christian values, my personal quest searches for the means of improving my mind and at the same time linking myself with a power source that is reliable. The longer I live the more I find some authority figures in my world want only to use my assets, for they themselves are weak and subject to evil influence.

Such was the dilemma of Deborah, a mother in ancient Israel, who lived when crime had infested her community. The engines of aggression growled on her national borders and life had become almost unbearable. The failures of the past were coming back to haunt her generation; they had not completed their God-given task of subjugating Canaan.

Matters of Most Importance

Deborah had an uncommon ability to see "the big picture." She confronted everyday affairs with sound advice, but she also insisted that her people ask the ultimate questions:

Who are we? (Not, what weapons do we have?)

Who are these other people? (Not, what will they do to us?)

Who is in charge? (Not, who is yelling the loudest?)

Every Israelite knew his heritage—a people redeemed from Egypt, led by Moses across the Red Sea and through the wilderness. Every day of that history had been a miracle. Under Joshua they had come into Canaan victors. Now it was different. Nobody living could remember knowing any of the founding fathers; they lived two centuries earlier.

Everything had changed—homes, marriage customs, religious life. Patriotism had waned. This was a new and frightening world with too much to tackle. Yet in spite of the depressing circumstances, Deborah saw hurting people, her countrymen cowering, leaderless. She saw the ferocious enemy; not his iron chariots but the commander of the charioteers. Her keen mind whirred with strategy.

Deborah's Design

Sisera was the name that terrified Israel. He was the villainous commander under Jabin, king of Hazor. Lying north of the Sea of Gennesarat (now Galilee), Hazor lay well within the borders of territory allotted to the tribe of Naphtali. Sisera's arrogance was enhanced by a slick fleet of nine hundred iron caissons pulled by thoroughbred steeds. His incessant posturing had all but halted normal life in the local villages and made travel on the main roads a rarity. Even the soldiers of Israel posed as harmless townspeople, lest they be attacked by Sisera's infiltrating guerrilla forces.

The lines in the ancient text seem to seethe with Deborah's impatience. Like an exasperated mother lining up her unruly brood, she spoke with authority, *Has not the Lord God of Israel commanded...?*

Her organizational eye fell first on the young man Barak. His family, headed by Abinoam, lived in Kedesh, right in the heart of the harassed tribe of Naphtali. She ordered him to round up ten thousand volunteers from his own tribe and their cousins from Zebulun. The plan: bivouac on Mount Tabor where they could command a view of the Kishon River valley below. God, she said, would lure Sisera into the valley, and they could swoop down and surprise him.

A Foray of Faith

Barak quivered. His people were peace-loving; all his relatives were into fishing and sailing along the coast—not making war. It had been years since any military maneuvers were held; their skills were rusty. No one would argue that danger existed, but... On the other hand, you didn't say "no" to a judge like Deborah.

If you go with me, I will go, but if you do not...I will not (Judges 4:8, NIV). Barak's courage obviously wavered at such an awesome assignment.

We women often forget how much influence we have. In our families we may feel it, but seldom do we exercise it for public encouragement. Deborah knew that her national welfare was in jeopardy, so she moved confidently toward obedience to God. Success was assured, since she had simply returned to the commands of God.

Down near the flat river banks the chariots churned along, but soon a thunderstorm slowed them. The chariot wheels were bogged down in the mud. With a grand finale of hailstones God held Sisera's army hostage to the onrushing Israeli ground troops. In a panic, Sisera himself abandoned his army and escaped on foot. The reader follows him, limping with exhaustion up to the tent of a woman named Jael. He knew her community had signed a pact with

Hazor, so he gambled on the fact that she would give him a friendly hiding place.

Jael seized this moment of revenge like a shepherd capturing a predator of his flocks. The narrative climaxes with her pretense of complicity. A cup of warm milk (actually a yogurt called "leben", often used as a sedative) was her tool. She put Sisera to sleep and hammered a tent peg through his temple. When Barak came by in pursuit of his oppressor, Jael calmly ushered him in to view the victim.

Such cruelty makes sense only in the context of that early-day Canaanite culture. Human desperation often resorts to savagery because preventive measures have so long been ignored. Our lesson from this pungent piece of history must focus on the heart and head of Deborah.

In accordance with near-Eastern custom, she recounted the exploits in Judges 5 and provides present-day women with a treasure chest of leadership principles:

1. *Teamwork.* Notice that she put Barak in the place of visibility. Male leadership was apparently deficient in her nation. Her nature was to speak up, to make things happen. But she understood the importance of men, and she was willing to share the glory of victory. She wisely enlisted and encouraged (perhaps even trained) a young man of potential. She also teamed up with him to record the epic as a duet. Together they sang their song.

2. *Praise to God.* Ultimately every success comes from the Lord (James 1:17). Deborah had a keen grasp of the components of victory. Look at her three-

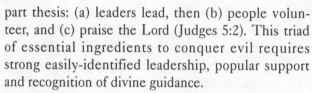

part thesis: (a) leaders lead, then (b) people volunteer, and (c) praise the Lord (Judges 5:2). This triad of essential ingredients to conquer evil requires strong easily-identified leadership, popular support and recognition of divine guidance.

3. *Obedience to God's commands.* The account of the battle continues to pay homage to God. It was not a pious overlay of religion, but a plan that integrated His wisdom and the prayer of His dependent people. Every detail of the war was effectively orchestrated by the Heavenly Commander, thus assuring victory.

4. *Awareness of history.* Knowledge of the past helped Deborah avoid the price of disobedience. Changing discouragement to the excitement of conquering the enemy is the stuff of progress. She taught hope to a new generation. Everybody got involved and the enemy was vanquished.

5. *Mature understanding.* Deborah prayed, *"May they who love you be like the sun when it rises in its strength" (Judges 5:31, NIV).* True leadership warms, cheers, arouses and nurtures every responsive seed. It strengthens because real leadership is servanthood with vision.

Our female minds crave information, but knowledge without character is destructive. Deborah's enemy was brilliant enough to have mined the iron ore from the earth and to manufacture death-dealing weapons. But the ways of God are far above man's schemes. The fear of God, said the wisest of all men, Solomon, is the beginning of knowledge.

As important as knowledge is, the human mind

must always be linked to its Creator to produce optimum results. This principle explodes from the natural creation. For example, the tiny little Blackpoll Warbler, which is smaller than a sparrow, flies annually from New England and eastern Canada on a non-stop, 2,500-mile trip, at altitudes up to 21,000 feet. The journey is possible because its respiratory system has a counter-flow of blood and air in its lungs that extracts oxygen from the atmosphere, enabling it to metabolize fat with remarkable efficiency. A professor at Swarthmore College plotted the little creature on radar, and declares it flies the equivalent of a man running a four-minute mile continuously for eighty hours.

The common hummingbird, beating its tiny wings at 3,000 wing beats per hour, exerts energy (per unit of its weight) ten times that of a man running at nine miles per hour!

Why is it important to connect with our Creator? *In Him are found all the treasures of wisdom and knowledge (Colossians 2:3, TLB).*

Our
Inconsolable World

❧

"Mister, ain't nobody lookin' fer me!" The words still haunt me although I heard them decades ago. They served as my early-warning for women's disaster in our nation. Late on a Saturday afternoon I asked my husband to get our younger son from the sandbox. I noticed through the family room window that Jimmy from down the street had come to join our Billy in his "highway construction" project for his toy cars and trucks. A verbal tug-o'-war was underway and it seemed to be a good time to clean up for dinner. When my husband told Jimmy that his mother was probably looking from him, he heard those words as the little pre-schooler left our back yard: *Ain't nobody lookin' fer me!*

If one wishes to take the pulse of a nation, or a church, or a home, he has only to peek into the nursery. How we care for our children is a vital sign of our overall health and a forecast of our future. Contrary to many heart-tugging pleas for aid, trouble is not a children's problem. It's a mothering problem. God composed His feminine symphony with a melody of nurturing. Any system, no matter the label, that allows women to bear children and not care for them is doomed to extinction.

Mommies Marching Home

Like the chronically ill patient, we have become numb to the sting of statistics, but not everyone has turned a deaf ear. According to the *Wall Street Journal*, more than 57 percent of American women serve in our commercial workforce, but many thinking women are frustrated. "Mommy wars" are raging and the pendulum is swinging in some places.[29]

For twenty years the *Yankelovich Monitor's* annual survey reported consistently that 30 percent of women would quit their jobs if they could get along without the money. But in 1991 it had grown to 56 percent. In Elmhurst, IL, a group calls itself FEMALE (Formerly Employed Mothers At Loose Ends), claiming 2,000 members nationwide.

As of 1985 one out of every six two-income couples with children under age six worked hours that did not overlap; they shared childcare. Split-shift parenting indicates that fathers are taking a more active role in parenting. Seventy-four percent of men in 1989 said they would rather have a "daddy track" job than a "fast track" job. This "father hunger" reflects perhaps their own unmet needs in childhood.[30]

Commendable as these trends may be, the ugly facts continue. Every year one million teenage girls, almost one of every ten, become pregnant.[31] The hype and glamour attached to sex and babies grossly distorts the realism of the hard work and heavy responsibility of bringing the next generation into our world.

Unfinished Agenda

In an excerpt from Dr. Benjamin Spock's book, *A Better World for Our Children,* he wrote:

Because of grossly inadequate high-quality day-care and the impact and influence of amoral and immoral television programs, the family has lost its dominant role...A first step in getting spirituality, love and kindliness back into the family is to cultivate them in marriage...I envy adult believers and their children for two reasons. First it gives them a moral and spiritual framework to support and inspire them. The second reason is more cultural. It is good for the children to get a sense of the background from which they have sprung...[32]

No matter where we dip into the home brew of our nation, we women are responsible for minding tomorrow. When the apostle Paul sent his young protégé, Titus, to pastor the church on the island of Crete, the society was in shambles. It is a mountainous island, some one hundred and sixty miles in length, but at most thirty miles across. Its many caves harbored pirates, and at the time the Roman government used it for military training maneuvers, as well as exile for its worst prisoners. Along with the military came thousands of slaves. Into this unlikely mix the gospel had been preached by Paul, and now Titus was assigned the task of building a leadership base.

Significantly, the apostle told Titus to teach the older men and the younger men. He was also to teach the older women but they were to teach the younger women (Titus 2:3-5). The curriculum included the loving care of their husbands and children, purity, self-control and primary responsibility for their homes. It matters not whether the problem exists in our own twenty-first or the first century A.D. God places daily care of the home and family into the hands that He created for the job.

Ancient Building Block

Zoom back to 2000 B.C. for an earlier version of the same story. Slave mentality is always developed by similar patterns: strip the male leadership, demand obedience to an impersonal authority, disregard personal dignity, limit individual choices. This unthinkable destiny had overtaken the heirs of the man of faith who trusted Jehovah, Abraham.

Isaac's son Jacob had twelve sons by four different mothers. His beloved Rachel bore Joseph, who was a contemplative boy, greatly disliked by his older half brothers. They sold him to Ishmaelite traders who took him to Egypt and there, after years of suffering, his brilliance earned him a position second only to the pharaoh. Because of his influence, he was able to rescue his father's family from starvation during a famine. Seventy of his relatives settled as shepherds in the choice grazing community of Goshen.

Generations later, after the Asian Hyksos had conquered Egypt and been subsequently ousted by the Babylonians, ruthless pharaohs spearheaded powerful armies north to the Euphrates River. No one remembered or cared about the former national hero, Joseph. His descendants were mercilessly put into slavery in a massive building program of temples and civic buildings to honor the ego of the pharaoh, probably the great Rameses II.

Levi's mother, Leah, was unloved by Jacob, a plight which enraged her (Genesis 29:31-34). The poet has truly written "Heaven has no rage like love to hatred turned, nor hell a fury like a woman scorned."[33] The Proverbs declares that one thing at which the earth trembles is an unloved woman who is married (Proverbs 30:23). Among that hapless group lived a family of unmatched courage. Both Amram and his wife Jochabed were descended from Levi, third oldest son of Jacob. They inherited a fierce spirit of resistance.

When the edict was announced commanding all new-born Hebrew boys to be placed in the Nile River as a sacrifice to the crocodile gods, Jochabed cried, "Enough!" To be sure she placed her beautiful infant son, Moses, in the river, but carefully cradled in a waterproof reed basket, close to the shore, watched over by his big sister, Miriam. Surely in her heart was a desperate prayer to Jehovah: If He was still there, would He please save her son.

History shouts God's reply to her faith. The world's greatest lawgiver, prophet and deliverer of his people, was born (Exodus 2:1-10), reared in the palace with an education equivalent to a combination of our law, medicine, military and government training (Acts 7:20-22). He was being groomed to become the next pharaoh. *Faith*, says Elton Trueblood, *is fear that has said its prayers.* Corrie ten Boom defines faith as *radar that sees through the fog to reality of things at a distance that the eye cannot see.*

God does not command us to restructure our political or economic system. He does declare that *without faith it is impossible to please God because anyone who comes to Him must believe that He exists and that He rewards those who earnestly seek Him (Hebrews 11:6, NIV).* The words of Dr. David Hamburg, president of the Carnegie Corporation, should stab the conscience of every mother today:

> *Failure to form a secure attachment to an adult in the first two years of life can hamper a child's learning as well as emotional growth.*[34]

Why are we doing everything else except taking care of our children? The major hurdle is not lack of money, but selfishness—doing our own thing, scrambling to find fulfillment in anything but what we do best: investing in leaders of tomorrow.

Modern science wears a black armband to mourn the explosion of the spacecraft Challenger ten miles above the Atlantic Ocean on a sunny Tuesday morning in January, 1986. Seven astronauts died in the tragedy, one of whom was a much-celebrated school teacher, Christa McAuliffe. Mass media blazed the story worldwide, lauding the pioneer spirit of this one civilian passenger-teacher.

Tucked away in that story, however, is a fatal flaw in our thinking, a discordant note, a disturbing error in our moral syntax. Our heroine was also a lawyer's wife, and the mother of two children, Scott, 9, and Caroline, 6. One had to search the back pages of the newspaper to discover this information because Christa was identified only by her profession.

Our Western world splashes its slogans boldly to the effect that children are our most precious resource, our priceless treasure. But with unanimous approval we chose her, one of more than 11,000 applicants, to fly this admittedly dangerous mission. For numerous reasons she could have been disqualified in the rigorous selection process. Physical health, intelligence, psychological well-being and a variety of technical skills were examined, but no one considered that being a mother was very important. Condolences were offered to the family, but that disastrous episode highlights a much deeper issue about our core values. What kind of a society is it that not only permits a mother of young children to place herself into a high-risk posture but celebrates her for it?

First Person

The centuries prior to the birth of Jesus Christ had dwindled to less than five when the great Persian monarch, Xerxes, one of the most illustrious of the ancient world, held a mammoth six-month-long feast to celebrate his intended aggressive sweep against Greece. Selling the campaign to his political and military chieftains was critical, inasmuch as his father had unsuccessfully attempted a similar expedition.

From the biblical record of this event, the Book of Esther, comes evidence that God directs women to perform leadership roles because of their divinely designed creative judgment. Amidst splendor and power, Esther moved with tact and resourcefulness. Xerxes, known also by his title, Ahasuerus, reigned over a region from India (the Indus Valley, now known as West Pakistan) to Ethiopia. Residing in this widespread dominion were large numbers of captive Israelites who had been displaced under the

Babylonian captivity. Some had been allowed to return to Jerusalem under their leader, Zerubbabel, to begin rebuilding the temple, but others remained.

Xerxes was living at his winter residence in Susa, two hundred miles east of Babylon, one of several Persian capitals, when the celebration of the intended offensive was held. The magnificence of the palace decor focused on the court of the garden where a climactic seven-day public banquet was held. Tapestries of violet and white linens hung between marble columns, held in place by cords of fine purple linen and silver rings. Couches of gold and silver were arranged on a dazzling floor of marble, mother-of-pearl and precious stones. Drinks were served in gold containers to everyone with no limitations.

On the final day of the lavish feast, the king sent seven chamberlains to bring beautiful Queen Vashti to him for display. Saturated with alcohol though he was, his word was law. Absolute dictators of modern times have no edge on the ancient monarchs. So feared and honored were they that only a few chosen slaves and select advisors were ever allowed even to see their faces. Power was derived from a mixture of royal bloodlines and military prowess, overlaid with religious intimidation. Of Xerxes' father, Darius I, one historian has written:

> He fought his way to the throne room over the bodies of those who opposed his right to rule. These men who wore the purple by virtue of the sword, rather than by the legality of inheritance, often mounted propaganda campaigns to legitimatize

their rule, to convince the people that they reigned by a right at least as great as that of lineage...to convince all men that only he was the chosen of gods and history to direct the destiny of the empire.[35]

Whether possible shame and humiliation awaited Vashti we do not know, but she refused to come and a public divorce was proclaimed. Undoubtedly she knew disobedience meant death, but in an almost contemporary type of display of women's rights, she rebuffed the king. The royal advisors reasoned that it could have sparked a rash of marital defiance in the homes of the people. Accordingly a law stating that *all the wives shall give to their husbands honor* was passed and the word dispatched throughout the empire. The wives were put in their places (Esther 1:20-22).

Fitting in perfectly with Xerxes' frame of mind, a beauty contest was subsequently contrived to search out the fairest specimen of womanhood to replace the banished queen.

Enter Esther

Mordecai was a Benjamite living in Susa, guardian of his uncle's orphaned daughter, Hadassah. His young cousin had assumed the Persian name, Esther, meaning "a star."

If Esther even had a question about what she would do with her life, it was soundly resolved by a two-pronged answer: tradition and circumstance! Her home training unquestionably cast her in the mold of a proud Jew, unwilling and virtually unable to bow to the corrupt and immoral gods of Babylon. Her future seemed to hang—together with that of her displaced people—in the greedy balance of Persian domination and eventual extinction.

In his "inaugural" statement unearthed by archaeologists, Darius I established his bloodline for five generations back, to make his point that royal blood ran in his veins.

> *But once again God intervened in a dark moment of history to show His power, to vindicate the words of Isaiah to Cyrus: So from the rising of the sun to the place of its setting men may know there is none besides Me, I am the Lord, and there is no other (Isaiah 45:6, NIV).*

Mordecai had a wild idea. Why not place beautiful Esther in the competition? He did, and, in contrast with the other contestants, she quickly revealed her remarkable upbringing. Her natural beauty, her personality and magnetism qualified her and, on Mordecai's advice, she kept silent about her Hebrew origin.

Preparation for ancient would-be queens was superintended by a retinue of maids who served the proper diet and assisted in grooming. A whole year was required before going to the king. The beautification consisted of a six-month regimen with oil and myrrh, followed by six months of spices and other cosmetics.

Myrrh is a gum resin from a tree-shrub growing in northern Africa. The fruit is smooth, somewhat larger than an English pea, colored variously from a reddish-yellow to brown or red, and the taste is bitter. Myrrh was used by the Israelite priests for holy anointing, for embalming (as was done to the body of Jesus) and as a drug when mixed with other herbs. Its use in the book of Esther was for purification. It was also an antiseptic, an astringent and a stimulant. For a woman to have close bodily contact with the monarch, she obviously had to be free of any disease or odor.

The second half of the make-ready included perfumes. Perhaps it was a kind of trial and error with various mixtures. At the time of her appearance before the king, the candidate could also receive jewelry to wear or other adornment. She was allowed to look her very best.

Esther astounded everyone by asking for nothing extra. She went before the king with, in the words of Peter, the ornament of *a gentle and quiet spirit. ...* The result was dramatic. It was love at first sight and he set the royal crown on her head. She found *favor and kindness*, most unusual since men in power were not known for benevolence.

The Weight of the Crown

The new queen must have known that the future of her race hung in the balance. Concealing her identity seems to show it was dangerous to be identified with Yahweh, the God of the Israelites. Whether Mordecai planned in advance to assault the throne through his cousin is not clear, but the idea that one alien subject could make a dent in that enormous bureaucratic Persian court is ridiculous. In fact, a whole debate could be waged over the situational ethics involved. Yet God allowed a miracle to be lived out.

Nothing sensational struck the court when Esther ascended the throne. As often happens in the lives of

God's children, the simple ebb and flow of man's affairs are used by Him to move His person into a strategic position. Not only had Esther's physical and temperamental loveliness propelled her far ahead of the competition, she went on to prove that she was mentally tough enough for a position of responsibility.

Without question God directs some women to step out of the home and family circle to assume a role of broader leadership. The professional woman shoulders heavy stewardship. Esther demonstrated her capability with distinction.

Treason in the Court

To the forefront of activity in God's flawless timing came the villain Haman. Vying for prestige and power, he was promoted to a kind of "big man on campus": the king *elevating him and giving him a seat of honor higher than that of all the other nobles (Esther 3:1, NIV).* Everyone bowed and paid homage to him, except Mordecai. As a god-fearing Hebrew and guardian of Esther, who was now close to the seat of power, Mordecai found this idolatry an impossible predicament.

Haman was descended from Agag, the infamous king of the Amalekites. As told in the Book of 1 Samuel, King Saul defeated this enemy, but disobeyed God in capturing the king along with the choicest animals. He disobeyed, he lied, and from the prophet Samuel he received the stinging rebuke: *To obey is better than sacrifice and to heed is better than the fat of rams (1 Samuel 15:22, NIV).*

Mordecai could not tolerate Haman. It was unthinkable that he, a proud son of Benjamin, should ever bow in deference to this uncircumcised Gentile. Such insubordination obviously set off a rage in Haman. He knew the Jewish heritage; to attack Mordecai openly would be illegal and unwise. His method would have to be underhanded.

Appearing before Ahasuerus, Haman convinced the ruler that there was a group of lawless people who should be removed. He even offered to pay well from his own pocket into the royal treasury to have something done about the matter. His apparent loyalty and concern moved the monarch so much that the ruler gave Haman his signet ring, a sign of complete authority to do as he pleased.

Dispatches were sent by couriers to all the king's provinces with the order to destroy, kill, and annihilate all the Jews, young and old, women and little children, on a single day…and to seize their possessions as plunder…the king and Haman sat down to drink, but the city of Susa was bewildered (Esther 3:13-15, NIV).

Haman shrewdly used the efficient Persian postal system so that the news would reach everyone simultaneously. His announcement set off complete despair. Mordecai's response was that of any stricken Jew; he put on sackcloth and ashes in mourning. What else? Other Jews joined him in fasting, weeping and wailing.

Esther was notified of her cousin's mourning but apparently did not understand the reason for it. In consternation she tried to send garments to him in order that he might come and talk with her, since she was not allowed to contact anyone in sackcloth and he was not permitted to pass beyond the palace gate. Her representative, however, brought back the bad news and with it Mordecai's plea that she intercede for her people before the king.

Such a suggestion posed a predicament for her, since no one could come to the king in his inner court unless he was summoned. The king had to hold out his golden scepter or the individual would be put to death. Mordecai's response:

> *If you remain silent at this time, relief and deliverance for the Jews will arise from another place, but you and father's family will perish. And who knows but that you have come to royal position for such a time as this (Esther 4:14, NIV)?*

Clearly this was a climactic moment in Esther's life and it required that she make a dangerous decision. It reminds me of Corrie ten Boom's book, *The Hiding Place*. When the Germans were killing Jews during the holocaust, her father was asked if he would be willing to take a Jewish mother and her baby into his home.

> Father held the baby close, his white beard brushing its cheek, looking into the little face with eyes as blue and innocent as the baby's…'You say we could lose our lives for this child. I would consider that the greatest honor that could come to my family.'[36]

Queen Esther had no way of knowing that at this juncture history was focused upon her. One can only imagine the rage that must have swept her as she read the edict and comprehended Haman's fiendish scheme. Her role became clear and she issued a request for all her people in Susa to fast for three days. *I will go in to the king, even though it is against the law. And if I perish, I perish (Esther 4:16, NIV).*

Weaving the Handwork of History

Surely her heart was pounding as the queen coolly appeared in the inner court with a serious face. The king asked what was troubling her, what was her request. Even to half of the kingdom would be given her. Her action was unprecedented as she extended an invitation for the king and Haman to come to a banquet she had prepared. It seemed to be an invitation on short notice, a kind of spur-of-the-moment luncheon date. The record shows that the king quickly found Haman, and the two were entertained by the queen. As they drank their wine, Esther felt the need for more time and asked them to return for the real banquet on the following day.

Haman was delighted. Although he was upset to see Mordecai as he left the palace, he went home and hastily organized a testimonial dinner for himself. To his wife, Zeresh, and his friends, he recounted how he had climbed the ladder of success. Clearly things were going his way. Imagine! Having dinner with the king and queen—how exclusive can a man get!

One thing remained to mar an otherwise perfect set-up—Mordecai. He was always there at the gate. When everybody else bowed down to Haman, next-in-command to the king, this Jew stood upright, staring insolently. You can almost hear him describing the scene in his sitting room full of worshipful friends and family.

Why get upset over one mere rebel? Build a gallows, suggested Zeresh, in a plot reminiscent of Jezebel (I Kings 21). Have Mordecai hanged in the morning. He will be out of the way and you can enjoy the banquet in the evening.

Heaven-sent Insomnia

Haman probably slept well that night. The conspiracy was working like a charm and he would be ready with his stinger for Mordecai at daybreak. But Xerxes had insomnia. He decided to catch up on his official reading and called for the chronicles and records of the court. As they were being read, a very interesting item popped up: two doorkeepers had surreptitiously tried to plan his assassination, but the murder was thwarted by a loyal subject named Mordecai.

Hmm-mm, wait a minute. *What honor or dignity has been bestowed on Mordecai for this?* He learned from the servant that nothing had been done. Such outstanding valor deserved a reward.

The next morning the king called in Haman just as he was arriving to discuss his hanging. Bursting with his unfinished business, the king asked, *What is to be done for the man whom the king desires to honor?* Exploding with ego and assuming that he himself was the honored one, he made an ostentatious suggestion. The man should wear a royal robe which had been worn by the king and ride on one of the king's horses in an elaborate ceremony to be held in the city square.

> *Go at once. Get the robe and the horse just as you have suggested for Mordecai the Jew who sits at the king's gate. Do not neglect anything you have recommended (Esther 6:10, NIV).*

What a turnabout! These words of the king probably left Haman speechless and shocked, but the plan was carried out by royal fiat. He rushed home to report the terrible news to Zeresh who added to his fears with the neighborhood gossip; namely, that the Jewish Jehovah could not be overcome. While she was speaking the carriage arrived for the banquet. Haman's web of intrigue had collapsed; he had no appetite.

Queen Esther had mastered the Persian court etiquette and hers was no small dinner party. It was a truly oriental feast of long duration, and not until the second day did she actually verbalize her request to the king. Her words, her timing, her self-control—all was carefully scheduled.

> *If I have found favor with you, O king, and if it pleases your majesty, grant me my life—this is my petition. And spare my people—this is my request. For I and my people have been sold for destruction and slaughter and annihilation...(Esther 7:3,4, NIV).*

It is, she was saying, only because mass murder is at hand that I bother you. Such electrifying news could evoke only one question: Who? The code of

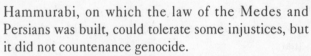

Hammurabi, on which the law of the Medes and Persians was built, could tolerate some injustices, but it did not countenance genocide.

For Haman the moment of truth was at hand. He could not hide any longer. Esther's dark eyes must have flashed with incriminating fire: *A foe and an enemy is this wicked Haman!* The record says that Haman became terrified.

As Esther's accusation sank into the king's understanding, he became very angry. Rising from his place, he took a walk in the garden. Suddenly he was befuddled. An old family skeleton had been yanked out of the closet and he needed fresh air to clear his mind.

History throws an interesting sidelight on the biblical record. Haman was clearly making a power play; probably aiming for the throne itself. Apparently the same thing had happened to his father, Darius. Xerxes was suffering the chronic problem of emperors—holding on to the reins of power.

Meanwhile Haman had fallen down next to Esther, begging for his life. When the king returned and saw him in this posture, his suspicions flared: *Will he even assault the queen with me in the house?* The royal words condemned Haman and before Ahasuerus was through speaking the servants had covered Haman's head with a hood for execution. The news that gallows were standing in wait for Mordecai was conveyed to the king, and he ordered Haman to be hanged on it. The sentence was swift.

Esther casts a long shadow into the twentieth century as a prototype for women who yearn to control their lives. Several principles are worth our consideration.

1. Be assured that God has put you where you are and that His timing is right. Trusting Him for the care He has promised his children is evidence of mature faith.

2. Take care of your body. It is our most precious possession, as Paul reminds us, *Do you not know that your body is a temple of the Holy Spirit, who is in you, whom you have received from God? You are not your own; you are bought at a price. Therefore honor God with your body (I Corinthians 6:19-20, NIV).*

3. Submit to godly home training and established authority. As Esther entered the palace she took with her an internal textbook, indelibly written in her mind and heart. Her early training was the best preparation she could have had for a position of leadership and public example.

4. Brains must accompany beauty. Leadership demands alertness and a teachable spirit. With all of our current opportunity for education, God seems to remind us daily: Learn! We have no excuse for ignorance.

5. Be an exemplary citizen. The only place where Mordecai disobeyed his king was when the local law conflicted with the first commandment. He could not bow to the wicked Haman. Obedience to the law should be part of our Christian testimony.

6. God has no restrictions on women aiming for the top in any field of endeavor. Just be sure your motives are right. Whether God privileges me to be a wife with primary responsibility to one man, or with broader stewardship, I must assume my job with courage and reliability.

Esther assumed a perilous posture, yet her risk

helped define the power of God. It elevated her to a new respect before her people. The Feast of Purim, remembered to this day by the Jews, commemorates her bravery and God's deliverance.

The woman to whom God entrusts influence over other people must take risks. Esther was limited by a strong male-oriented society and she faced a sinister foe, but she remained totally feminine, using the resources God had provided. Like Queen Esther, we can fearlessly face any opposition if we have made the basic decision: Serve Jehovah at any cost. He always honors the bravery of faith.

This ancient episode is more than a bone-chilling drama. We bask in our rich heritage of privilege and dignity, enjoying the highest level in history for women of legal, educational and social status. Have we forgotten that we are indentured slaves to our Creator who bought us with His life from the sin market? The eighteenth-century wisdom of Edmund Burke is in order. "History," he said, "is a pact between the dead, the living and those yet to be born. We dare not ignore or trivialize the legacy, nor are we free to negotiate our stewardship."

The old fable of the hunter and the bear illustrates our danger: With his rifle cocked at the charging bear, the hunter heard the furry beast suddenly cry out, "Wait, don't shoot! What is it you want?"

"Well, I was just looking for a fur coat," said the hunter.

"Oh, is that all? I am so relieved," replied the bear. "All I wanted was a simple meal. Let's work something out; surely we can negotiate." So for quite a while they talked and negotiated. Finally the bear stood up and walked away. He had his meal and the hunter was wearing a fur coat!

Part Four

HOW CAN GOD'S WOMANHOOD FIT ME?

THE JEWEL
Because of her strategic placement in society, woman functions as the keeper of the keys to stable civilization.

THE MANAGER
A woman's managerial skills are versatile and clever, able to wreak havoc or bring order to her world.

THE BEAUTICIAN
A woman's connection with her sensual nature opens the door to burgeoning beauty or gross degradation in her own and others' lives.

THE INVESTIGATOR
When the female mind embraces faith in God, the potential product is staggering; conversely, her inordinate persistence of data for selfish purposes is overwhelmingly destructive.

THE CAREGIVER
No touch to a needy person is as welcome as that of a caring woman; but the same touch turned against someone can be insufferably cruel.

THE CONTROLLER

God's womanly creation has unlimited means of control, but they must be tied to His principles for beneficial consequences.

Making Life Work

With impish flair someone has written that in the big workshop of life there are two types of people: those who know what to do with their ratchets and flanges, and the others who can't get the workshop door open. Estelle, our prototypical American woman in the first chapter, obviously is multi-talented, skillfully keeping her life in order. She mixes childcare and adult interests with apparent ease; she manages a home, a career, a marriage and a private mindset that hungers to advance in life while at the same time enjoying it.

People and procedures tend to blur in her swift current, but she maintains her poise. Occasionally she secretly wishes she could run away, and at other times she stifles a primitive urge to grab people by the throat and yell, "Listen to me, you idiot!" Both extremes are, of course, brief flashes of human frustration. All she can do, really, is fit into the routine—or is it? Let's re-visit her.

Estelle is sorting through the day's mail. Dressed in a soft green robe, having bathed Stephanie and put her to bed with warm hugs, she tried to place a phone call to her father, as requested, but his line was busy. Now her attention is drawn to an envelope addressed to her, Ms. Estelle Coolidge, from the corporate headquarters of her firm. Why would they be sending something to her home address?

Dear Ms. Coolidge:

As you are aware, our Board of Incorporate Members recently held their annual review of our leadership team. We are happy to report substantial growth…

Her eye skipped to the next paragraph:

We are pleased to announce that your name was submitted for advancement to full partnership in the firm…

"Mama Stel?" A tiny, plaintive voice at the kitchen door interrupted her. There stood Stephanie, crying, definitely sucking her thumb, holding a bedraggled stuffed rabbit. Estelle sensed trouble, a sudden regression to infant behavior. The toy had been a beautiful soft, yellow Easter gift named Sunny Bunny, given to Stephanie by Doug just before his honeymoon with Estelle. Somehow the little girl derived comfort from it and only recently had been persuaded to place what was now called Saggy Baggy Rabbit in the back of her closet.

"Well, Steffie, darling. What's the matter?"

Stephanie opened her fist. "My tooth came out. I want my Daddy!"

Estelle gathered her up on her lap and wiped her tears. With a soothing, yet bright, voice she said, "This is very exciting. It shows that you are growing up! You've lost your baby tooth, and you know what? Some people say that if you put it under your pillow, something very special will happen in the morning. Let's go do that."

Back between the sheets, Stephanie persisted in asking why her Daddy could not be home. Summoning her best caretaking skills, Estelle sat down on the bed. "You know, when I was a little girl like you, my grandmother told me once that little girls have to learn that some things we do not like can never be changed. It's very important for Daddy to be at his office tonight, and it does not mean that he does not love us. But my grandma also told me that God sees into our hearts and knows when we are sad. She taught me to pray to Him because He hears us and He gives us everything we need—not everything we want, but what we need. Would you like to pray to Him?"

Stephanie nodded and Estelle asked her what she would like to pray for. With great intensity, the child replied that she had something very special, so Estelle told her to pray. Without hesitation, Stephanie closed her eyes. "Dear God, Mama Stel said you listen to us. So I want to tell you that I miss my Daddy very much, and also I would like to ask You if maybe you have an extra baby we could have, so I won't feel so sad. I really need a baby sister or even a brother."

Opening her eyes, she asked her astonished step-mother if that was enough. Assuring her that it was,

Estelle kissed her and left the room. Back in the kitchen she sat stunned and a bit confused. Years before she had gone to Sunday school and church, but prayer had not been a part of her life for many years. Now suddenly reminded of God, she felt small and vulnerable.

Again Estelle dialed her father and reached him. Could she come for a visit, he asked. He wanted to discuss his will. He felt it was time to talk about her mother's welfare after he was gone. No, his health was fine. Yes, he had been on the phone earlier, talking with his brother...Estelle heard the garage door open and concluded the conversation.

Doug burst through the door, dropped his coat and brief case, and scooped up Estelle in his arms. "My beautiful one, you will never guess what happened. Honey, this is wild! You know why Jean LeBois came today? You'll never guess!"

Doug's eyes were sparkling. He put her down, kissed her forehead and cupped her face in his hands. "The company wants me to take over the Northern European office—*how would you like to live in Paris, Madame!?*"

Pursuing a Worthy Goal

Upward mobility, success, affluence. These magnets are perhaps more dangerous than their opposite labels: failure, poverty, disaster. Our womanly desire to maintain control of our lives assigns prosperity to a high-risk category. Estelle's overload of blessings demands careful steps through the maze of her complicated life.

How does she know the right way? To whom can she afford to say no? What is a legitimate use of her resources and energies? If ever she needed a working relationship with her Creator, it is now. She cannot risk a wrong turn.

Just as surely as Eve in the garden sowed her own seeds of misery in an effort to act independently of God and of her husband, so we women today will suffer hardship if we insist on living our lives with disregard for divine guidance, or if we downgrade the provision God has given to women in Christian marriage.

James, the New Testament writer who translated theology into weekday rules of conduct, posted this advice:

> *Now listen, you who say, 'Today or tomorrow we will go to this or that city, spend a year there, carry on business and make money.' Why, you do not even know what will happen tomorrow. What is your life? You are a mist that appears for a little while and then vanishes. Instead, you ought to say, 'If it is the Lord's will, we will live and do this or that' (James 4:13-15, NIV).*

The control factor, that dire warning given to Eve on the brink of her expulsion from the garden, stands today as possibly the most potentially damaging instrument of destruction in the female arsenal.

Your desire will be for your husband. God lit the warning light: Beware of your fervent nature that drives you to take charge when God has provided male leadership! With your outstanding management skills, with your unerring eye for elegance, your thirst for knowledge and your instinctive talent for caregiving, you have the capacity to destabilize your home and your society. Or, as a talented shock absorber, you can ease tensions.

Because of our twentieth-century advances in education for women, we naturally have opportunities to step into positions of authority. It is, therefore, especially vital to remember God's priorities. At all costs He must be honored; marriage must be respected and the next generation trained. Our friend, Estelle, faces life-altering decisions—for herself and her loved ones. Hard choices come packaged with God's blessings, and we women of unprecedented good heritage are accountable to Him.

The good life can easily camouflage our need for supernatural direction. Not only does placing our lives in God's hands remove the pressures of decision-making; it allows us to learn how protective our Heavenly Father is. He asks only that His children come in faith, willing to follow His leading. If we let Him design the pattern, the finished product will someday be perfection. Listen to lines of the anonymous poem, *The Weaver*:

> *My life is but a weaving between my Lord and me,*
> *I cannot choose the colors He weaveth steadily.*
> *Oftimes He weaveth sorrow, and I in foolish pride*
> *Forget He sees the upper and I, the underside.*
> *Not till the loom is silent And the shuttles cease to fly*
> *Shall God unroll the canvas*
> *   And explain the reason why.*
> *The dark threads are as needful In the Weaver's*
> *   skillful hand*
> *As the threads of gold and silver*
> *   In the pattern He has planned.*

Manager's Mindset

◆

ohn Larroquette, prominent television personality, once stated, *I wanted to be either an actor or a priest... they both sell fantasies.*[37] Strangely, for many people faith does not seem to fit anywhere in accounts receivable, but with God's ingenious wisdom it can translate to assets on the bottom line.

After consulting for fourteen years with various Christian organizations, Bruce Cook concluded that planning without faith was the norm. A Christian with a Harvard M.B.A., he set abut explaining how the two work together in his book, *Faith Planning*. Too many of us fail, Cook decided, either because we do not plan at all or we plan improperly. Like Eve's seeing the fruit as useful, we have a worthy objective, but we have a flawed means of reaching it.

Without God in the equation many of us look at our resources, calculate what has happened in the past, and set a goal for the future based on a given percentage of increase. Projection—it seems rational.

Others piously decide to "trust God." We go out on a limb, usually with a credit card, and pray that God will supply the payments. That is not faith; it is wishful thinking. Neither projection planning nor wishful planning taps into God's resources. We must plan by faith, a scriptural process with four distinctive steps, each of which requires an answer to a specific question:

1. *Why?* What is the purpose for being here, doing what we are proposing? The Bible enlightens:

I know the plans I have for you, declares the Lord, plans to prosper you and not to harm you, plans to give you hope and a future. Then you will call upon me and come and pray to me, and I will listen to you. You will seek me with all your heart (Jeremiah 29:11-13, NIV).

Do not be anxious about anything, but in everything, by prayer and petition, with thanksgiving, present your requests to God (Philippians 4:6 NIV).

If any of you lacks wisdom, he should ask of God who give generously to all without finding fault, and it will be given to him (James 1:5, NIV).

The first step is to examine your purpose by verbalizing it in prayer, the most basic act of faith. Then think, discuss and listen for His leading.

2. *What?* Now it is time to set goals, faith goals. Whenever we pray, we must base our request upon His will. Believe that He will do what is best for us at this time, in this place, for these people. What do we want to accomplish? The second step is to set direction

and focus; a concrete framework for our plan. For example, notice the competence of Nehemiah, the brilliant engineer, in specifically planning and carefully assigning tasks as the wall of Jerusalem was rebuilt (Nehemiah 3).

3. *How?* No goal can ever be accomplished without strategy. Step three is to structure elements which must be built into the plan in order to be successful. The book of Titus illustrates this principle. In order to establish viable leadership in a morally deteriorated society, Paul instructed Titus to teach certain individuals according to a prescribed pattern.

4. *When and if?* This fourth step implements or translates the strategy into a schedule. Only with proper procedure will the goal be realized. The final week of the life of Jesus Christ on earth was carefully programmed. His triumphal entry into Jerusalem, His confrontation at the temple, His judiciously scheduled dialogue and parables all preceded the sorrowful trek to Gethsemane. In His excruciating arrest, crucifixion and glorious resurrection in three days, God Himself demonstrated perfect planning for the greatest event of all ages (Luke 19-23).

Our first mother was mesmerized by the fruit because it was helpful for her planning, but her plans went awry. She omitted God (and her husband) from her plan of action. Many of us grasp the ornaments dangling in our private universe, and find ourselves with unmanageable problems. The good news is that we do not have to stagger under the load. Jesus Christ came to relieve us.

Come to me, all you who are weary and burdened, and I will give you rest. Take my yoke upon you and learn from me, for I am gentle and humble in heart and you will find rest for your souls. For my yoke is easy and my burden is light (Matthew 11:28-30, NIV).

In our brutal environment how can the light touch of gentleness and the sweet fragrance of humility prevail? In our raucous uproar who can ever hear kind words or find time for rest in our rough and tumble struggle for survival? The secret lies in the right connections, a private line to serenity. Taking Christ's yoke and learning from Him provides interior fittings for our souls.

Sometimes gentleness must be very persistent; sometimes humility requires an extremely firm hand. Our world will not tolerate wimps. True Christianity never teaches a cowardly, weak-kneed lifestyle. The Christian woman proceeds confidently because her plan of action has the Master's seal of approval.

The Beauty
of Faith

❧

Thirty-six-year-old Jacquie had been in fashion
merchandising for seventeen years—a beautiful and
classy high-end consultant. A woman would come to
her shop, for example, and hand her a cruise schedule.
Jacquie would plan an appropriate wardrobe hour by
hour. She knew she was telling women how to look
beautiful on the outside, but she often saw ugliness
underneath and quietly wondered what to do about it.

Through a radio ministry, God reached into her
inquiring mind and made Himself known. Alone in her
apartment she accepted Jesus Christ as her personal
Savior. Then just a few days later a man walked into
her shop late on a Tuesday evening in October. He
locked his arm around her neck, put a knife to her
throat and said he was going to kill her.

A quiet calm came over me. I prayed silently
and knew that Jesus was standing right there

beside me. I replied, 'It's OK if you want to kill me, but why? I'll be going to heaven. Will you have that kind of peace when you die?'

The man became enraged, and although he did not rape her, he beat her unmercifully. He fractured her skull and pulled out clumps of her hair. She has twenty-two puncture scars where he stabbed her.

I was bloodied and bruised from head to toe, but I just kept repeating, 'Jesus! Jesus!' At the hospital the nurse who took my blood pressure was shaking at the sight of me. She could not believe my BP was normal. My mother almost fainted and my father went 'bonkers.' Everybody was shook up—that a white, Caucasian female in a good neighborhood could have been attacked like that.

Even though she looked horrible, Jacquie felt well and asked to be released to go home.

I stood in front of my full-length mirror and surveyed my naked body. Out loud I thanked Jesus and said to him, 'I feel beautiful for the first time in my life. When they beat You, You must have looked something like this.' Within two weeks I was healed, even though the doctor had predicted a six-month rehabilitation with prolonged physical therapy.

Jacquie told me this story in Palm Springs, California, where I saw her with the ugly scars on her neck, but with her value system well intact. She now works with quadriplegics, marketing their paint-by-mouth pictures. Her words to me were emphatic: *"Tell them, Jeanne, please tell them that women must be beautiful inside; they must look like Jesus Christ to speak for Him."*

Her words are indelibly etched in my memory. Jacquie understands that beauty comes only in imitating our Savior. Beauty contrived to highlight human ambition is at best shallow prettiness. True loveliness of the spirit is a gift only from the Creator.

Those who visit the Grand Canyon in Arizona are awestruck by its grandeur. Measuring 277 miles long, a mile deep and nearly eighteen miles wide, the canyon changes colors constantly. As morning moves toward evening, the hues change from red to gold to pink to orange. As night falls purple shadows come and the almost-incomprehensible vastness of the scene engulfs the spectator with a peculiar loneliness. Carl Sandburg wrote: *There goes God with an army of banners.* The effect overwhelms our finite senses.

Earthly beauty, exhilarating as it is, can be only a faint reflection of God's true majesty, which no human mind can absorb. The apostle John's magnificent description of Heaven in the Revelation leaves us teetering on the edge of our imagination. Only with resurrected bodies will we be able to appreciate it, but in our present finite body God re-creates a foreshadowing.

Beauty and the Best

Married women of faith have the high privilege of blooming into beauty. The apostle Peter commanded wives to submit themselves to their husbands and pursue a kind of spiritual make-over, *the unfading beauty of a gentle and quiet spirit…of great worth in God's sight.* This elixir of love (1 Peter 3:1-4) promises that husbands can actually be changed by observing purity and reverence in their wives.

If this is so, we must ask the question, what is submission—really? As most of us perceive it, it is demeaning and leads to bitterness. But this command is given by both apostles Paul and Peter. It is a military term which means to rank below. The imperative form is used and the verb is reflexive; that is, we are commanded to submit, but we must do it ourselves. No one else can make us submit.

When this truth is combined with Paul's teaching in Ephesians 5, commanding a husband to love his wife, the sense can be better understood. I, as a wife, must obey God first so that I trust Him for changing my husband. But it is not a matter of "You win, I lose" or "You're right, I'm wrong; I'm weak, you're strong." It is a win-win agreement. We both win, because I choose to cooperate, to submerge my wishes for the good of our loving relationship. That choice requires a stout heart. But when a husband knows that his wife consistently respects and honors him enough to conform to his wishes, even against her better judgment, his love is unleashed.

All of this almost-too-good-to-be-true transformation happens, Peter and Paul say, when a wife exercises her will to obey God concerning her husband. It is no small feat to reverse a stubborn, self-indulgent man, as many have discovered. Nevertheless, the

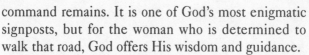

command remains. It is one of God's most enigmatic signposts, but for the woman who is determined to walk that road, God offers His wisdom and guidance.

Because Christian marriage is pivotal in family success, the old enemy from Eden is still at work. Paul wrote that marriage is a mystery (Ephesians 5:32); it is the earthly picture of God's Son loving His bride, the Church. Some day He will take her to live with Him forever. No better place for Satan to scramble the Good News!

The downward drag against true beauty pulls heavily in our world, but when a woman allows divine beauty to shine through her, the effect is stunning. Wives are not the only ones commanded by God to submit.

Submit to one another out of reverence for Christ (Ephesians 5:21, NIV). Submission is to be the lifestyle of every believer. There is something about a strong, self-directed woman voluntarily, lovingly cooperating with clear-eyed vision that solidifies a home, a community and a nation. It models respect for authority; it breeds tranquillity; it pleases God. This kind of inward beauty is available only from the Source, the Creator who is the essence of truly exquisite loveliness.

Knowing
and Believing

&

*E*very baby, male and female, is born into our world with an inordinate need to learn, to find out who and what is important. It is necessary for mental stability, for a sense of identity. But as a girl grows into a woman, she increasingly develops a curiosity about the world of power, man's domain. The book *Games Mother Never Taught You* by Betty Harragan[38] illustrates this interest. It provides a kind of road map for women who have entered the corporate world of work, an explanation of language and symbols and expectations. We women suspect that somehow something is going on that we don't know about, and we are desperately eager to find out.

Historically, education for women has lagged behind that of men. As late as 1925 the average girl in America left school in the ninth or tenth grade. Sometimes she worked outside the home, but more often she stayed home with her mother until she got married. In the middle and upper classes it was not considered proper for her to leave home. Not surprising, then, is the passive helplessness that became fashionable for women. Our recent explosion of feminism seems to be a reaction to that mindset.

Women Divided

In a recent issue of the national student newspaper, *Campus*, a junior at Utah State University, Emily Fisher, reviewed the book, *Who Stole Feminism*. She wrote, "A hundred years ago women were fighting for the right to learn math, science, Latin—to be educated like men; today many women are content to get their feelings heard, their personal problems aired, their instinct and intuition respected."[39]

Current momentum among young women seems to press deeper into the why's of social behavior. The issue has in fact divided feminism into the so-called equity feminists and the gender feminists. This latter group is accused of institutionalizing the idea that women are hapless and helpless. Equity feminists, on the other hand, want a level playing field for both women and men.

If it is true that female students are questioning the feminist story of the gender war, what is it truly that a woman wants? Some exasperated men will dismiss the question with *"She doesn't know what she wants."* And he is probably closer to the truth than most of us women would like to admit.

The words of Grumpy, one of Snow White's seven dwarfs, said it for many men: "She's female, and all

females is poison! They're full of wicked wiles."
Asked to explain wicked wiles, he replied: "I don't
know...but I'm agin 'em."

Believing this popular gender put-down easily
leads us to feel somehow deprived. Add that negative
tug to our normal desire to learn, and we display an
almost-savage competitive spirit.

But, undoubtedly, we want *something* more. Just as
there was in Eve's sinless mind a pull toward the fruit
because she believed it was desirable for gaining wisdom, every woman has a nagging certainty that a further bit of knowledge will complete her understanding
and make life sensible. We are mentally itching.

Wisdom and the Female Mind

Our good fortune is that God who programmed our
thinking knows our inside need. The apostle Paul
spoke eloquently to the point:

> We, however, speak a message of wisdom among the
> mature, but not a wisdom of this age, or of the rulers of
> this age, who are coming to nothing. No, we speak of
> God's secret wisdom, a wisdom that has been hidden,
> and that God destined for our glory before time began
> (1 Corinthians 2:6-7, NIV).

Since the apostle wrote those words, two millennia
have elapsed and nothing new has come from human
thinking. We in the Western world still operate on the
basis of Greek philosophy. It has provided the under-
pinnings of all of our industrial and electronic inven-
tions. Secular minds still churn in quest for missing
pieces.

What is the custom-designed portion that will sat-isfy a woman's utilitarian, beauty-loving, inquiring mind? I am convinced it is a relationship, not detached theory. The only way to quench our inner discontent is with soul-satisfying solutions. When Jesus Christ gathered his disciples in the upper room just prior to his crucifixion, He calmed their fears with an incredible promise. He would not leave them as orphans in a hostile world:

If you love me, you will obey what I command. And I will ask the Father, and he will give you another Counselor to be with you forever—the Spirit of Truth (John 14:15-17).

This group of eleven diverse disciples had united around His leadership. Although they were men of extreme opposites politically, ethnically and tempera-mentally, they were as one in their dedication and devotion to Him. He had drawn them and trained them and was now leaving them in a love relationship that stretched them far beyond human feelings. God the Creator cares enough about mankind to intervene with a personal resolution and rationale for each life that will receive Him. The missing ingredient for the seeking woman is the certainty of truth. More factual knowledge simply promotes more questions, but the wisdom of God settles the soul's private dust storm. Because He knows us intimately, His wisdom is tai-lored to our own psyche. He freely gives it in ex-change for our trust and obedience, but too often we distrust and disobey.

Wandering Alone

Linda Jo never finished high school. She was a pretty girl, intelligent, but boys attracted most of her attention. Before she was out of her teens she was pregnant, then married. Her low-salaried husband depended on his parents for nearly everything, including the house trailer in which they lived. His night watchman job kept him gone for long hours and Linda sank into an addiction to soap operas and fast foods.

Pregnancies continued and by the time she had three children, she sought out help from a local church. Sadly, the people there who taught the Bible neglected to meet more than superficial needs. She met some women who babysat occasionally and tried to include her in social events, but Linda Jo's excess weight and lack of skills in almost every area drove her to loneliness and desperation.

An old high school friend had divorced and moved to Montana. Once in a while she would write a letter, and in one of them she invited Linda Jo to visit. The invitation planted an idea, and in her bleak distress this young wife contrived to steal her husband's car, to empty his bank account and with her children head out some 2,000 miles for Montana.

I do not know the sequel to the story, but I do know there are thousands of Linda Jos every day screaming for something more in their lives. The problem is not just a question of self-esteem; and is far more than a lack of formal education. Linda Jo was a woman crying out for a way to still the storm inside of her. She needed an older woman to love her, to teach her virtue, self control and how to care for a husband and a family (Titus 2:4). Most of all she needed to serve God supremely, not herself.

The biblical writer, James, distinguishes two kinds of wisdom. One is heavenly and the other we all know well. Earthly wisdom yields envy and selfish ambition that leads to all kinds of disorder. But the wisdom that God gives forms a splendid, multi-faceted gem. Its soft radiance appears passive because it is peace-loving, considerate, sincere and humble. Do you recall *The Pilgrim's Progress*?

And what is this valley called? We call it now simply 'Wisdom's Valley'; but the oldest maps mark it as the Valley of Humiliation.[40]

Learning through Loving

True wisdom comes through adversity, but its strength is like the hardness of a diamond and it cuts through our world's slippery, double-dealing façade. Wisdom from God exudes purity, insists on submitting to God's will, acts bravely with mercy and fierce impartiality (James 3:13-18).

History teems with wise women who refused to let their lives die on our society's unproductive vines. At the turn of the century, Jane Addams established Hull House, offering a network of personal, supportive relationships to unmarried women. Later, Lucy Mitchell dedicated herself to intelligent, caring development of the children of working mothers.[41]

Hundreds of women have learned foreign languages and left their homes in order to reach and teach women and children in every part of the world.

Mary Slessor of Scotland committed herself to the women of Nigeria and won the confidence and respect of both the Nigerian and British governments. She organized their court system and became a vice consul, mediating between the two governments. Amy Carmichael of Ireland gave fifty-three years to young, grossly-exploited orphaned girls in South India. Her wisdom was not of this world. She wrote:

> The devil does not care how many hospitals we build, any more than he cares how many schools and colleges we put up, if only he can pull our ideals down and sidetrack us on to anything of any sort except the living of holy, loving, humble lives, and the bringing of men, women and children to know our Lord Jesus Christ not only as Savior but as Sovereign Lord.[42]

Eve was not wrong in desiring wisdom. She was deceived into thinking she could obtain it by circumventing God's plan. To be truly wise, a woman must learn from His Spirit and to let God give her away to other people.

High-Yield Investment

A rich young ruler sadly turned away from Jesus because he was unwilling to sell his possessions and give money to the poor, as Jesus had told him. One of the watching disciples volunteered, *"We have left everything to follow you. What then will there be for us?"* It was true; Peter and his brother had changed careers. They had left a lucrative fishing business for a life of personal deprivation in a traveling ministry of healing and helping, learning from Jesus of Nazareth.

After drawing Peter's attention to an eternal perspective, the Son of God clarified the long-term value of sacrificial giving: *Everyone who has left houses or brothers or sisters, or father or mother or children or fields for my sake will receive a hundred times as much and will inherit eternal life (Matthew 19:27-29, NIV).* One cannot give anything to God without receiving many, many times over blessing and reward.

Caretaking, that quality of women first introduced in the book of Genesis, condenses into an act of giving. Just as true wisdom reaches its highest application in teaching God's truth, so a woman's investment of her unique skill of nurturing must flow toward soothing, relieving and lifting up others. That is what we woman do best.

Little girls tend to be fuss-budgets. I remember reading about the studies of boys and girls at play. When a dispute arose, little boys argued and haggled for approximately five to seven minutes, then chose up new sides and continued the game. When the little girls disagreed, they argued and quibbled and bickered, on and on, until finally they drifted off, each with a new best friend, never to resume team play. We women define ourselves in terms of relationships; we judge ourselves by our ability to care. We try to change the rules in order to preserve people connections.

These conclusions were examined by Harvard researcher Carol Gilligan,[43] and she concluded that we women are at risk in our society which rewards separation. Our identity and intimacy conflict; integrity and caring at times seem to clash.

What happens then, to the Christian woman who is programmed—but not practiced—for caretaking? She convinces herself because of overwhelming social pressure that children, elderly and ill persons, unfortunate people with disabilities and a host of other needy folk are not on her priority list. She is "not the motherly type."

Non-Mothers

The answer to that question was given hundreds of years ago to other women of privilege who, like us, turned away from whole-hearted nurture and the tending of their domestic scene. Listen to the scathing words of the prophet Isaiah:

The women of Zion are haughty, walking along with outstretched necks, flirting with their eyes, tripping along with mincing steps, with ornaments jingling on their ankles...In that day the Lord will snatch away their finery; the bangles and headbands and crescent neck-laces, the earrings and bracelets and veils, the head-dresses and ankle chains and sashes, the perfume bottle and charms, the signet rings and nose rings, the fine robes and the capes and cloaks, the purses and mirrors, and the linen garments and tiaras and shawls (Isaiah 3:16-22, NIV).

With finely detailed sharpshooting, the prophet draws a bead on the women's wear of that day. These Israelite women were delinquent in their duties of home and family; they had neglected the outstretched hands of their community. They would, he said, find themselves branded as slaves, dressed in sackcloth, with shaved heads living in filth. Their men would be killed in battle and they would sit mourning on the ground yearning in vain for a home and a husband. Harsh, shocking words, but not just ancient history, these are the words of the inspired Scriptures, spoken by the Almighty God Who never changes. We can never afford to turn our nurturing skills solely upon ourselves.

Outstretched Hands

Women of the Western world, we must wake up to our God-given responsibilities. God does not take lightly our dereliction of duty. He has commanded us to care for our children, to tend our homes and commit ourselves to our husbands. We are charged to look after the widows and orphans, to feed the poor, to patiently love and look after the elderly and the sick. We are commissioned for hands-on involvement.

Gina did that. She was a barmaid in south Bronx, street-smart and playing the numbers racket to help pay for the kids' clothes. Her health was not the best; she had had throat surgery and her headaches were severe, so she decided to stop by a tent meeting, even though she really thought all preachers were con artists. When she got there no seats were vacant except in the first row, so she sat down, heard the Gospel and went forward at the end of the meeting.

The preacher prayed for her and she went home. Amazingly, her headache was gone. For six nights she went back, filled with a peace and a strange joy she never knew before. When she was asked to stand on street corners and hand out tracts, she talked to the derelicts who told her over and over, "Ain't got no place to eat 'n sleep."

Gina found herself telling them to wait right there and she would take them home. Her husband and kids thought she had flipped her lid. But she told the Lord that since He had done so much for her, she wanted to do something for Him. She found a church where the Bible was believed and lived out; subsequently she went to Bible school and eventually Gina Huddleston established a full-fledged care center for hurting and abandoned people.

It is more blessed to give than to receive. These words fell from the lips of the One who gave His life. They were quoted by the weeping Apostle Paul in his emotional farewell to the elders of the church at Ephesus. His final charge to them: *We must help the weak (Acts 20:35).* This investment of sharing with those who lack yields highest returns, not only in fulfillment, but in eternal rewards.

But wait, God said to Eve that she would have pain in child rearing. It would cost her dearly to exercise her nurturing gifts. Giving oneself always involves sacrifice, but it is what we women do best. Why should we squander our noblest gifts on transient targets when we can build into the lives of people who last forever?

One question nags: *How can I do it with everything else in my life? I'm exhausted trying to meet all the demands!* This is where good management serves us well, where teamwork shines, where wisdom guides us. And for us Isaiah has a word of comfort:

> *The Lord is the everlasting God, the Creator...He will not grow tired or weary...He gives strength to the weary and increases the power of the weak...those who hope in the Lord will renew their strength. They will soar on wings like eagles, they will run and not grow weary, they will walk and not faint (Isaiah 40:28-31, NIV).*

The Faith Enigma

❧

As a little girl I often visited my country cousins with a blend of pleasure and terror. Tom was a year older than I, with red hair and an abiding passion to find ways to scare this timid little city gal out of her wits. One of his favorites was the swinging bridge. My uncle had hung a flexible steel span with boards across his creek, which ran between the barn and a field where he grew grain for the cattle. Tom always had something over there to show us, a tree house or a nest of rabbits. He would run ahead and stand on the far side and wait until I got part way across. Then he would grab the cable and swing it from side to side, all the while yelling for me to hurry up.

High over the rushing stream I would hold the slim wire handrail and freeze with fright, begging him to stop. The more I pleaded the harder he laughed and taunted me as being a dumb, no-nothing green-horn girl from the city. After one such heart-stopping episode I begged my father to do something about Tom.

Very calmly he told me that I was the only one who could stop him. How? Very simple. Don't look down at the water, don't just stand there and yell, focus my eye on the big tree trunk where the bridge is hooked and walk straight toward it. Like walking on air!

When Tom was not there I went out and practiced. Dad's advice worked like a charm. Never again did I fear the swinging bridge.

In somewhat the same way God is our immoveable tree trunk, our point of balance. He has written for us His secret for a life free from paralyzing terror.

> *Let us fix our eyes on Jesus, the author and perfector of our faith, who for the joy that was set before Him endured the cross, scorning the same, and sat down at the right hand of the throne of God...so that you will not grow weary and lose heart (Hebrews 12:2-3, NIV).*

In our sensuous world, we fuel most of our days with feelings, many of them unwholesome and harmful. But we were intended by our Creator to be not only creatures of feeling, but souls with a conscience toward God. When ill health, grief, or any personal loss smashes us to the ground, we must know that He is allowing that pain to mold us into the image of His Son, who suffered and thereby learned obedience (Hebrews 5:8). With His presence assured, our feelings absorb hope like green grass after a spring rain.

Sparkling Sylvia, who reminded me of Marlo Thomas, drove me in her BMW to the San Jose airport. She told me that she had worked to put her first husband through law school. After he gained his credentials, he went to work five days every week in San Francisco and "played around," then came home and taught Sunday School, and acted like a good husband and model father. One evening he told her he was having an affair with his secretary. The next morning he left for good.

So devastated was Sylvia that she resigned from all her church activities and gave herself to prayer and personal Bible study while at the same time working to support her little girl. For one year she re-examined herself in the light of God's standards, seeing herself not as a rejected woman but as a much-loved and highly-prized daughter of the King of Kings. She promised God that whatever He brought to her she would hold lightly. She centered her energies on giving Him the glory.

Then she met Kurt, very casually. Not since they were twelve years old had she seen him, but he recognized her and they chatted when she was picking up her daughter at Sunday School. Would she be free for dinner? His wife had died in an auto accident and he had a little boy. Their friendship grew into love and marriage. God delights to restore joy to the sad of heart. Sylvia understands that God allowed her pain in order to produce the praise that she now gives Him constantly.

Daughters of the King

Many Christian women see themselves as ragged paupers instead of privileged daughters of the King.

My own self-confidence had never been fed and watered. I learned to become invisible in threatening situations and was very grateful when God gave me a witty, self-assured husband who fronted for me—at first. I often explained myself as a "private person." Then, through studying the gospels, I began to understand that God wants to make me like Jesus Christ, and He was very much a people person. What was I to do? Social contacts panicked me. Two verses from the Living Bible have transformed my life.

The first one comes from Paul's mentoring words to the young and timid Timothy: *For the Holy Spirit, God's gift, does not want you to be afraid of people, but to be wise and strong, and to love them and enjoy being with them (2 Timothy 1:7, LB).*

How could I make this happen? People intimidated me, especially sophisticated strangers. To quell my fears, God led me to another bit of advice from Paul, who was certainly an expert with people: *Be honest in your estimate of yourselves, measuring your value by how much faith God has given you (Romans 12:3, LB).*

It was like a blank check. God tells me to do a self-exam and assign a value, however much I am willing to trust Him. Now I understood why Paul could state with boldness *I can do everything through him who gives me strength (Philippians 4:13, NIV).* The basic question is, do I really believe that I am the daughter of Eve, highly valued by the Creator, the crowning jewel of God's creation? I must be, or Jesus would never have come to earth and died for me.

Like Eve, we wrestle with decision-making—the choice of a mate or a house or whether to accept a certain job or political involvement. We struggle with money management, infertility, adoption problems and disappointment in our families. Seemingly trivial, but important, irritations such as car repairs, intrusive neighbors or my unmanageable hair or a leaky roof are chronic reminders of our mortal weakness. How can I act like a princess when I have to live like a scullery maid?

The Past: Our Preparation

We began this capsule of Christian womanhood in the Garden of Eden. This place of Paradise reveals our roots physically, intellectually and spiritually. After the Fall things went downhill rapidly, and we traced the drama in the lives of some of Eve's daughters, watching in wonder as they attempted to make life work as a woman. For a good reason these important episodes have been preserved for us. Paul wrote, *These things happened to them as examples and were written down as warnings for us...so if you think you are standing firm, be careful that you don't fall (1 Corinthians 10:11-12, NIV)!*

In order to set our own course for the future, gaze once more back into Eve's beginnings.

It was the wedding of all time. God the Father presented His daughter of dazzling charm to the man of perfection He had made. With unrestrained exuberance Adam took her to himself and found her to be utterly alluring and nourishing to his single self. He had not known what he was missing. Now she was there to stimulate and animate. Her provocative presence lifted his life to unimaginable bliss. With purest passions aflame, the two possessed each other.

God gave them His eternal blessing and pronounced their union very good.

If we could somehow return to Eden, armed with our biblical briefing, and follow that ravishing bride to her rendezvous with the crafty impersonator of evil, we would cry out desperately *"No! Don't eat it! Please, don't..."*

But she did. Eve was a woman of action, as are her daughters. Exuding her God-given urge to respond to beauty, to manage her surroundings, to gain more wisdom, she ate the forbidden fruit and then gave it to her husband.

As spiritual death began its slow, withering assault on the guilty pair, the heavy-hearted Father did what He had to do. With grief that only a holy God can know, He led the stricken sinners outside their luxurious garden abode. He could no longer trust them in Paradise.

The Genesis account alerts us to God's specialty—making people. After all of the beautiful things He made previously as scenery and preparation for His center-stage star, the Divine Creator made man and from him a woman. After Eden, He became a specialist in re-creation...

> *Therefore, If anyone is in Christ he is a new creation; the old is gone, the new has come (2 Corinthians 5:17, NIV).*

Process of Re-molding

Travel with me across the years to the sorrowful town of Bethany during the time when our Lord was here on earth. Approximately two and a half miles southwest of the city of Jerusalem, it lay within the district where King Herod had put to death all the baby boys aged two years and under, in an effort to stamp out the life of the King who had been born in Bethlehem.

The dusty little village was home for a man named Lazarus and his two sisters, Mary and Martha. Because it is also near the Judean desert where John the Baptist preached, quite possibly the family looked eagerly for the Messiah he announced. When His disciples were sent out in advance of Jesus' ministry, they probably came to this home, and thus the incident recorded by Luke (Luke 10:38-42) highlights what happened as the Lord taught there.

With her characteristic love of entertaining, Martha, probably the older sister, issued the invitation for the Lord and his disciples to come for dinner. Her organizational skills evidently made her an extraordinary hostess, and for this occasion she went all out. Mary, with a quieter, contemplative temperament, sat at Jesus' feet and listened intently to what He said.

Something went wrong. Martha lost her poise and tried to implicate her sister by accusing her of negligence. Mary should have been helping, she told the Lord. In response Jesus rebuked Martha. He told her that only one thing is necessary; that is, simplicity is in order when He is present. Mary had chosen wisely to learn from Him.

The reader does not know anything more about this family until John records in his eleventh chapter that Lazarus became terminally ill. Although the sisters sent for Him, He delayed His arrival for several days in order that God would be glorified. When news of His approach came, Martha hurried out and walked with Him into town. If He would just have been there, she said, Lazarus would not have died. Jesus could have healed him.

The Savior's words to her both comforted and enlightened: *Your brother will rise again.* Yes, she responded that she understood that eventually He would. Jesus continued:

> *I am the resurrection and the life. He who believes in me will live, even though he died; and whoever lives and believes in me will never die. Do you believe this (John 11:25, NIV)?*

Jesus was giving Martha a theology lesson, but she did not score very high. Yes, her theology was orthodox, but her application was faulty. She could believe for the future, but what about today? She needed help now!

When Jesus came to Mary, she could barely speak because of her grief. Jesus made no attempt to teach her. He understood and wept with her. Then He went to the tomb of Lazarus. He commanded that the stone be rolled away.

Martha, the fastidious hostess, recoiled with embarrassment. The body had been deteriorating for four days; the stench would be most offensive!

Then came the words of our Lord to her:

> *Did I not tell you that if you believed, you would see the glory of God?*

Martha's utilitarian womanliness, her delicate aesthetic sensitivity and her keen need to understand all, clouded and hindered the simple faith the Lord wanted. In a resplendent display of His awesome power, Jesus Christ proceeded to pray to the Father and then to command Lazarus to come forth from the tomb. For Mary and Martha faith was galvanized.

A most instructive sequel follows. John records in the next chapter that, although the Jewish leaders were seeking Him for arrest, Jesus fearlessly accepted an invitation to dinner at the home of Simon the Leper. Undoubtedly the host was an ardent follower of the Lord and since His healing from the dread disease, he had re-entered society and wanted to demonstrate his loyalty. John records that *Martha served*. Of course Martha served; she was the town's most qualified hostess. But this dinner party was different because of Martha's servant heart. Her self-serving spirit had succumbed to newness of life and love for Christ.

Mary was also there, and she was also a re-created person. She wanted to express her deep devotion to the Lord with her dearest possession. Perhaps it was meant for a dowry, for it was equivalent to her life's savings, worth approximately a year's wages. We know only that she took an alabaster jar filled with pure nard. It would have been just over ten ounces, the stopper sealed with wax. She opened it and poured it on the Lord in an act of worship. Evidencing her humility, she let down her hair and wiped his feet, much to the consternation of the watching disciples.

The gospel writer, Mark, records that Jesus rebuked the men for their criticism. He understood that this was an act of unparalleled adoration. She would, He said, be remembered for all time because of it. Mary had heard, and heeded, His teaching. She had walked through the valley of the shadow of death and found Him there sharing her tears. She had believed Him and she had witnessed His power. Now she would give Him, in worshipful love, the very best that she had.

Reason to Serve Him

Can you comprehend the enormity of what God did when He created you as a woman?

God could force us, man or woman, to obey Him because we are His by creation. He owns us by sovereign right.

Do you understand the all-encompassing love of an omnipotent God who reached down into time and space to rescue you from the enemy of your soul?

When His Son, Jesus Christ, died on the cross and was resurrected from the grave, God demonstrated His love and redeemed us. He paid the price to buy us back from the slave market of sin, to heal the rift from the rebellion of our headstrong parents, Adam and Eve. On the basis of that redemption He could force us to obey Him on legal grounds, but He did neither one.

God's appeal to mankind is purely on the basis of personal love. Although He owns us by creation and He legally possesses us because He redeemed us, nevertheless He implores us to love Him, and in return He bestows the spirit of Christ, the Holy Spirit, the third Person of the Trinity, to indwell us as a guiding compass. Then we begin to find wisdom, a tailor-made ability to distinguish right from wrong, to love other people and to exercise good judgment in portraying our individuality.

Are you aware that your feminine nature is very precious to Him, and are you spiritually astute enough to bend your will to His love and to let Him re-create His life through yours?

The Last Word

～∽～

The wonderful but mysterious world of women touched my youngest years first through my troubled mother, then through my wise and caring paternal grandmother. Finally, I met my first real girl-person, my brilliant next-door neighbor with whom I played school. Since I was a year older, I was always the teacher, but she, a future high school principal, challenged and argued. Unwittingly she taught me much to admire and appreciate—and question—about my opposite gender.

As I reflect on Jeanne's writing about women of honor, those rudimentary days reappear. Then I had no basis in fact for the strong nurturing, resistance and even manipulation I felt. Now these Scriptural insights help to clarify and classify, to legitimize what the male mind tends to stow away as imponderables. It's like knowing what's under the hood of my car; appreciation grows with knowledge.

My own study of the Scriptures long ago led me to understand that God's creation of woman was an extraordinary gift to the man. When I married Jeanne, I began to experience first-hand the wild roller-coaster ride of every new husband. Ecstasy nose-dived occasionally into agonizing wifely reasoning. I have cherished her dearly; I have coached and cheered her, but I cannot claim to have understood, except as God has opened our understanding of each other. As a well-worn husband, father and grandfather of nearly a dozen females, I find in her diagnosis on these pages some refreshing reaffirmations:

• This study affirms femininity as a creative gift of God.

• It moves women from a defensive to an offensive mindset, galvanizing them to become the unique persons He created.

• It should motivate women to commit themselves to a modeling role, to mentor and teach the next generation.

• Knowledge forces responsibility. When a woman understands who she is, then she is accountable to God to be a fully-functioning female.

• We all need to go to school on these women found in the Bible, to learn the principles they teach about the inscrutable man-woman puzzle that baffles so many of us.

Now that my wife has explained herself to me, the question is, can I understand her? Fortunately for me as a husband, God requires only that I understand and obey His Word. There He commands me to love

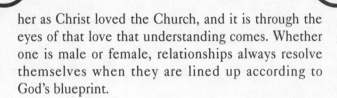

her as Christ loved the Church, and it is through the
eyes of that love that understanding comes. Whether
one is male or female, relationships always resolve
themselves when they are lined up according to
God's blueprint.

Howard G. Hendricks

Endnotes

1. Margaret L. Coit, "The Sweep Westward," *The Life History of the United States*, Vol. 4 (New York; Time-Life Books, 1963), p. 88.

2. Paula Stern, *The Atlantic Monthly*, March 1970.

3. Cited by John Bartlett, *Familiar Quotations* (Boston: Little, Brown and Co., 1955) p. 728.

4. Francis Schaeffer, *Genesis in Space and Time* (Downers Grove, IL: InterVarsity Press, 1967), p. 6.

5. C.I. Scofield, D.D., ed., The New Scofield Reference Bible (New York: Oxford University Press, 1967), p. 6.

6. Joseph C. Aldrich, *Secrets to Inner Beauty*, (Portland, OR: Multnomah Press, 1977), p. 19.

7. Edward J. Young, *Genesis 3* (London: Banner of Truth Trust, 1966), p. 16.

8. Roy B. Zuck, *Barb, Please Wake Up!* (Wheaton, IL: Victor Books, 1983).

9. Stephen B. Clark, *Man and Woman in Christ* (Ann Arbor, MI: Servant Books, 1980), p.11.

10. R.K. Harrison, "The World of Genesis and the Patriarchs," *Zondervan Pictorial Atlas*, E.M. Blaiklock, ed. (Grand Rapids, MI: Zondervan Publishing Co., 1969), p. 142.

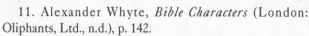

11. Alexander Whyte, *Bible Characters* (London: Oliphants, Ltd., n.d.), p. 142.

12. *New York Times*, 12/3/93, p. A25.

13. Judith Herman, M.D., *Training Directory, Victims of Suicide Program* (Cambridge, MA: n.d.).

14. Robert D. Foster, *The Challenge*, (Colorado Springs: NavPress, 1981).

15. Quentin J. Schultze, et al., *Dancing in the Dark* (Grand Rapids, MI: William B. Eerdmans Publishing Co., 1991), pp. 56-57.

16. Carl Rowan, *The Dallas Morning News*, Field Enterprises, 9/13/76.

17. Blaise Pascal, *The Mind on Fire*, James M. Houston, ed., (Portland, OR.: Multnomah Press, 1989), p. 135.

18. C.F. Keil and F. Delitzsch, *Biblical Commentary on the Old Testament, Volume I*, "The Pentateuch," translated by James Martin (Grand Rapids, MI: William B. Eerdmans Publishing Company, 1949), p. 103.

19. Lillian Schlissel, *Women's Diaries of the Westward Journey*, (New York: Schocken Books, 1982), p. 15.

20. Joy Jacobs, *They Were Women Too*, (Harrisburg, PA: Christian Publications, 1981), Week 52-Saturday.

21. *American Demographics*, July, 1991, p. 36.

22. Elizabeth Wayland Barber, *Women's Work: The First 20,000 Years* (New York: W.W. Norton, 1994), p. 29.

23. *Science*, "The Making of a Female Scientist," 12/17/93, p. 1315.

24. Sally Hegelsen, *The Female Advantage* (New York: Doubleday, 1990).

25. Sam Levinson, *In One Era and Out the Other* (New York: Simon and Schuster, 1962), p. 23.

26. Doris Kerns Quinn, *Modern Maturity*, Oct-Nov, 1987.

27. William J. Bennett, *The Book of Virtues*, (New York: Simon and Schuster, 1993), p. 14.

28. Blaise Pascal, *op. cit.* Chapter X, p. 77.

29. *Wall Street Journal*, July 23, 1993, p. 1.

30. *Perceptions.* 9/20/94.

30. American Medical Association Report, n.d.

32. Benjamin Spock, *A Better World for Our Children*, cited by *Denver Post*, 2/26/94.

33. William Congreve, "The Morning Bride," 1697, cited by John Bartlett, *Familiar Quotations* (Boston: Little, Brown & Co., 1955), p. 298.

34. David Hamburg, *Time*, 3/23/92, p. 59.

35. Bernard Goldman, "Politicking in Ancient Persia," *Natural History*, April, 1976, p. 36.

36. Corrie ten Boom, *The Hiding Place* (Grand Rapids, MI: Zondervan, 1972).

37. John Larroquette, "NBC's Night Court," *USA Weekend*, July 25-27, 1986.

38. Betty Harragan, *Games Mother Never Taught You* (New York: Warner Books, 1977).

39. Christina Hoff Somners, *Who Stole Feminism?* (New York: Simon and Schuster, 1994).

40. Wayne Martindale and Jerry Root, *The Quotable Lewis* (Grand Rapids, MI: Tyndale House, 1989), p. 612.

41. Joyce Antler, *Lucy Sprague Mitchell* (New Haven, CT: Yale University Press, 1987).

42. Elisabeth Elliot, *A Chance to Die* (Old Tappan, N.J.: Revell, 1987).

43. Carol Gilligan, *In a Different Voice* (Cambridge, MA: Harvard University Press, 1982).

Study Guide

For Your Consideration

Recognizing that a single volume can only begin to explore the complexity of the female creation, this study guide is intended to lead you into a closer look at the biblical truth of each chapter.

There is an additional study section on each page. This section does not tie in with the chapter content but instead focuses on the six distinctives of womanhood that have been woven throughout this book. Prayerfully allow the search light of the Holy Spirit to illumine your mind with a clear recognition of how you demonstrate each distinctive.

If you use the study questions for a group, it is important to consider how others perceive you and how closely your self-evaluation reconciles with others' opinion.

When you complete each distinctive, set constructive, measurable goals for correction or modification and share that goal with a friend.

Through Female Eyes

Page 19

1. Why do you sometimes feel your dreams are dissolving and hopes shattering?

2. Describe the difference between the world's view of a successful life and a woman's view of meaningful fulfill-ment?

3. From deep within your heart, what words do you long to have God whisper to you?

∽

Additional Study

THE JEWEL

Eve was created and positioned by God as His crowning jewel of all that He had made. She was, therefore, the prime target for the tempter. Satan has not changed his tactics. Women continue to be tempted just as Eve.

1 Corinthians 10:13
List general areas of temptation in your life.

James 1:13-14
Identify the human weakness that could cause you to give in to temptation.

Galatians 5:16-18
Describe personal strengths or resources you may access to allow you to overcome each specific temptation.

Woman: God's Crowning Achievement
Page 25

1. When you first thought of yourself as a woman, what was the national mood about women?

2. How do your desires for womanhood conflict with prevalent ideas of the nation? How do your desires conflict with the prevalent ideas of the church?

3. How do you feel about the author's statement, "...for with Eve the pulse of humanity begins to beat"?

❧

Additional Study
THE MANAGER

Woman wants what works. She naturally organizes her life to yield a profit.

1 Samuel 25:1-17
Abigail was a lovely woman with an alert mind. God was her source of true joy. What specific qualities can you identify about Abigail that enabled her to survive?

1 Samuel 25:18-31
According to Hebrew custom a woman was not to give counsel except in an emergency. Abigail waited for the appropriate moment. What circumstance in your life needs changing? How can you use Abigail's example?

Morning of Purity
Page 31

1. Adam was alone. What word pictures come to mind when you think of the word alone?

2. In your own words, describe the identity that God gave woman in Genesis 1:26-28 and Genesis 2:18-25.

3. How does this identity help you discover that you are a Woman of Honor?

Additional Study
THE BEAUTICIAN

Woman is built for beauty. She is naturally beautiful and she is stirred deeply when true loveliness touches her.

Describe the most beautiful landscape you can imagine. Do you think your description would be exactly like anyone else's? Doubtful...

1 Peter 3:3 & 4
What two descriptions of beauty are found in this passage? Do you have a preference? Does God?

Spiritual Suicide

Page 37

1. What areas of your life cause you the most dissatisfaction?

2. How does dissatisfaction open the door to temptation?

3. Look up the following verses and write out steps to resist temptation: Proverbs 3:5,6; Romans 8:28; Philippians 4:6-8

∽

Additional Study

THE INVESTIGATOR

The urge to know more is a primary drive within a woman and because of it she is vulnerable to deception.

Romans 16:18
Flattering words may cause us to draw wrong conclusions. Can you remember a time when you believed what you wanted to believe because it was flattering, not necessarily true?

Colossians 2:4
Paul warns us to beware of persuasive words. Marketing people are clever with persuasive words. What was the last item you bought that did not live up to its claims?

The Moment of Truth
Page 45

1. Describe the feelings associated with words like guilty, damaged, condemned and ashamed.

2. In contrast, describe the feelings associated with words like forgiven, restored and accepted.

3. Read Romans 8:35, 38, 39. Once we have received Christ as Savior and asked forgiveness for our sins, nothing can separate us from His love. What area of your life needs this assurance today?

∽

Additional Study
THE CAREGIVER

A woman's need to nurture energizes her relationships with a caring spirit in spite of obstacles.

Psalm 91:1-16
Understanding and accepting the care of God for us equips us to care for others. List specific ways that God has demonstrated His care for you.

Psalm 51:12-13
Because you are so beautifully cared for, identify someone needing care and plan specific ways to reach out to that individual.

The High Cost of Living Outside Eden

Page 51

1. Think back to a time of disappointment in your life. Although it is not necessary to share the circumstances, describe the feelings you were experiencing.

2. Whenever we enter the emotional valley of tragedy and disappointment, a thousand questions surface. What questions are we likely to ask about ourselves? What are we likely to ask about God?

3. What are some truths you know about God that will help in hard times?

∽

Additional Study

THE CONTROLLER

Woman strives to take charge, concentrating her many capabilities on leadership goals, but apart from God's enablement she is frustrated.

Genesis 24:12-26
Rebekah was in control of her destiny only as she acted according to God's plan. Identify the specific leadership qualities demonstrated by Rebekah.

Genesis 27:1-17
Rebekah recognized the spiritual dimension in Jacob's life. History records that Rebekah was more concerned with Jacob's prosperity than his character. How can you give direction for someone's ultimate good and not violate God's moral laws?

Finding the Jewel

Page 61

1. There is no higher honor bestowed upon womanhood than that of being created in God's image. What characteristics can be seen in women that reflect God's attributes?

2. How do these same characteristics manifest themselves when they are distorted by sin?

3. God wants to unearth the jewel He created in each woman. How can imitating Christ help us discover the incredible plan God has for our fulfillment?

Additional Study

THE JEWEL

God's highest purpose for His beloved daughters lies in her exquisite capability to reproduce herself in other lives, an infiltration of love and goodness to men, and as a tutor of what is best in life for children and other women.

Titus 1:8
Name someone who has influenced you, and describe how they influenced you.

2 Thessalonians 3:6-9
2 Corinthians 3:1-5
Identify ways that you can influence others with direct personal contact.

The Manager
Page 67

1. What happened when Eve and Sarah tried to override controls that God had put in place? How can their experience help you when you become impatient and want to take matters in your own hands?

2. Read James 1:2-4 and Romans 3-5. How does God build perseverance and faith in our lives?

3. The angel asked Hagar, "Where did you come from? Where are you going?" How would you answer these two questions?

℘

Additional Study
THE MANAGER

Normal impulses provoke a woman to organize and nail down her personal life. Under divine control she is stunningly effective at pacing, balancing and stabilizing her world.

Philippians 4:11
Hebrews 13:5
Our culture places women in a position requiring a great deal of balance. We must work diligently to keep 'needs' and 'wants' in perspective. Create a list with two columns, NEEDS & WANTS. Carefully think through the items for your list and try to include all dimensions of your life.

The Beautician

Page 77

1. Read God's description of two kind of wisdom in James 3:13-18. What proves that Abigail had "wisdom from above"?

2. Truly, Abigail knew God. David acknowledged who had sent her. Does your attitude reflect a heart committed to God and His purposes? List areas in your life that need balance and identify specific steps to establish balance.

3. Read again the last paragraph on page 85. What beauty shines through your life?

∽

Additional Study

THE BEAUTICIAN

Deeply touched by her senses, a woman tends to act in response to what she perceives from her sensory guidance system. Women's intuition is a valuable gift from God. Identify specific ways your "intuition" has influenced your decision making process.

Psalm 119:10-16
How can God help you understand your role as a woman?

Psalm 119:17-24
Identify areas in your life where you act on intuition. How often are you right?

The Investigator
Page 87

1. When Naomi left her homeland she faced the future with hope...but instead found bitter disappointment. What encouragement can be drawn from Naomi's life when we experience grief and sorrow?

2. As friends, mother-in-laws, neighbors, co-workers...we have the opportunity to be light shining brightly in the darkness. Summarize principles from Naomi's life. Prayerfully consider which of these you should apply in your own life.

3. As a woman with many opportunities—what priorities, what habits, what words need to be changed so others will find in you a faith so strong that they are compelled to say, "Your God will be my God"?

Additional Study
THE INVESTIGATOR

Fear and natural inhibitions are overridden by a woman's insistent drive to discover additional details which could be of use to her.

Judges 4:1-11
Deborah is recorded in the Bible as a fearless patriot. Her trust in God allowed her to act with confidence. What details do you think Deborah needed to make her decision prior to going to battle with the Canaanites?

Psalm 73:24
Consider a personal situation you face—investigate the facts and list Ephesians 3:20 your response and what you think God's response would be to each fact.

The Caregiver

Page 99

1. How can Hannah's example influence your prayer life?

2. Read Hannah's song in 1 Samuel 2:1-10. Make a list of the attributes of God found in these few verses.

3. What are some practical ways a woman who has never had children still display God's gift of mothering?

୬୦

Additional Study

THE CAREGIVER

All of the feminine leanings toward stability, gracefulness and inquisitiveness seem to converge in to a natural ability to provide personal attention to anyone in need.

1 Samuel 1:7-18
Hannah is frequently described as the woman who personifies ideal motherhood. Perhaps her vow to God equipped her with determination. What qualities do you learn from Hannah that you should cultivate in your life?

1 Samuel 1:22-28
Hannah kept her vow. Have you promised God something? Our God is faithful and longs for us to be faithful to Him. Fulfilling her vow must have brought Hannah great sorrow. What do you face in your life that is not easy? Trust God for strength and record your progress with praise.

The Controller

Page 113

1. Think of relationships and opportunities where you have influence. How can you be sure you are leaving a legacy that builds rather than destroys others.

2. In what situations are you most likely to use manipulation or deceit rather than trusting God?

3. When you feel God's eyes looking in sadness on your actions, what can you do to turn that look of sadness into one of joy?

∽

Additional Study

THE CONTROLLER

The opposite gender always presents a challenge to the female psyche. Instinctively she covets the opportunity to outwit him, but unless he is supernaturally disposed to regard her with respect she loses equality.

Genesis 27:18-29
Rebekah was a creative woman. Could she have used another method to accomplish her desired result?

Genesis 27:30-46
Rebekah had outwitted Isaac and grief followed. Choices have consequences and some choices have long-term consequences. Can you identify areas in your life that are the result of long-term consequences of choices you have made?

Getting God's Viewpoint

Page 119

1. Read 1 Corinthians 10:11. What positive changes would you like to see in your life as a result of what you are learning from this study on womanhood?

2. What is your best strategy for these changes to become a reality?

3. We all long to hear expressions of restoration and love. Read again the paraphrase from the prophet Hosea. Which words mean the most to you? Why?

Additional Study

THE JEWEL

If a woman understands who she is in divine perspective, she can move herself into her rightful position of royalty by allowing God to take charge of her life.

The need for someone to take charge of our life can become clouded in the busyness of day to day living. Review your daily schedule and prioritize your activities.

Colossians 2:10
Identify specific areas in your spiritual life to develop.

1 Peter 2:9
List the advantages identified in the suggested scripture that come to you as a believer.

Woman in Charge
Page 123

1. Considering the biblical accounts of Lydia, Deborah, and the Proverb's 31 woman, why is there tension between women who work at home and those who choose careers outside their home?

2. What often happens to the spiritual life of a woman who is competent in managing multiple projects? In practical terms, how can this be avoided?

∽

Additional Study
THE MANAGER

Putting her own life in order is a natural womanly inclination, but for success she must follow biblical guidelines for jumping the hurdles.

Romans 12:19-21
Contemporary thought teaches that self-fulfillment is a necessary first step before we can 'manage' or bring order to our world. How can you be prepared to act with self-control? If you are married, managing our life takes on new dimensions. Despite the sin nature, marriage reflects God's protection plan for women. Think about various ways your husband manages your life and how that affects your own management.

Beauty Is Not For Sale

Page 127

1. Honor and humility often defy one another and yet God desires we embrace both. How do we find the right balance?

2. Read the qualities of real beauty listed in the last paragraph on page 128. What would you add?

3. Describe the happiest time of your life. Describe the saddest time. How has God used these circumstances to fashion beauty in you?

✍

Additional Study
THE BEAUTICIAN

Her preference for prettiness will be crushed unless a woman allows the Lord Himself to open her eyes to see His version of beauty.

Proverbs 11:22
Define discretion.

Isaiah 28:1
How have you been influenced by our culture in you definition of beauty?

A Nose For Good News

Page 133

1. Are you finding it difficult to relate to Deborah? Read her story and song in Judges 4 and 5 and find several principles that you can use in your own life.

2. What concerns do you have for our nation or your community that are strong enough for you to take action? What action will you take?

∽

Additional Study

THE INVESTIGATOR

Dead-ends abound in our world's data-base, but God's promise of His Spirit to teach a woman about life makes every day an exciting prospect.

1 Corinthians 2:9-16
Do you have a dead-end? Describe the elements that created the dead-end and search for answers. Ask the Holy Spirit for guidance in your search.

Our Inconsolable World

Page 141

1. What child or adult do you know who might be saying, 'Ain't nobody looking for me.' How can you help?

2. Describe your childhood. Was it lonely or secure? How are your childhood circumstances impacting your life as a woman?

3. What is testing your faith today? What do you need to do to trust God for the outcome?

Additional Study

THE CAREGIVER

The womanly instinct for tending to other people with concern is ready-made for this world's ills, but only when she exercises the touch of the Master will she experience indescribable fulfillment.

Romans 15:1-2
Galatians 6:1-5
Do you know someone who is weak—perhaps in their walk with God? What can you do to strengthen that individual?

Galatians 6:9-10
Have you given up on a task? think about what caused you to give up and try again. Fulfillment comes with accomplishment.

First Person

Page 149

1. 'History is a pact between the dead, the living and those yet to be born.' What does this mean to you?

2. Which qualities do you admire most in Esther's life? What practical steps can you take to develop them in your own life?

3. For what cause would you be willing to say, 'If I perish, I perish'?

∽

Additional Study

THE CONTROLLER

Living as a woman in a man's world lends itself to unbearable disappointment, except that God has provided for woman His ingenious method of excelling beyond circumstances.

Ruth 1:6-14
Paul describes Naomi as a 'desolate' widow. Women had no means of economic support. What advantages would Naomi have today?

Ruth 1:16-22
Ruth maintained a poise in her grief and that strength influenced her mother-in-law. In circumstances out of her control she acted with determined purpose. What circumstances in your life are out of control? How can you positively effect change in that circumstance?

Making Life Work

Page 167

1. List what you consider your five greatest strengths and your five greatest weaknesses.

2. Is it easier for you to admit your strengths or your weaknesses? Why?

3. An 'open door' is not always an opportunity from God. How can you know His will when facing decisions?

Additional Study

THE JEWEL

Because of her strategic placement in society, woman function as the keeper of the keys to stable civilizations.

Deuteronomy 6:6-7
List ten successful people that you know. How did their mothers influence them?

2 Timothy 1:5
How can you be encouraged by the influence Timothy's mother and grandmother had on him? How does it motivate you?

Manager's Mindset

Page 173

1. What are the differences between wishful thinking and faith planning?

2. Think of a goal you would like to achieve in the next six months. Now answer the four distinctive questions mentioned in this chapter: Why? What? How? When and if?

3. If you feel weary and burdened, what is preventing you from responding to Christ's gentle invitation to 'come, take, learn'?

❧

Additional Study

THE MANAGER

A woman's managerial skills are versatile and clever, able to wreak havoc or bring order to her world.

Proverbs 16:28
Think about your mental library of information. Do you know things about family members or friends that you need to commit to prayer and not discuss?

1 Timothy 5:13
Proverbs 11:11
Name specific ways you can manage information about others without violating confidences.

The Beauty of Faith

Page 177

1. List five women you admire. What qualities make them lovely?

2. Choose one woman from your list who best reflects faith in Christ. Explain why you chose her.

3. Would you be listed among women who others admire? If yes, why? If no, how can this change?

❧

Additional Study

THE BEAUTICIANL

A woman's connection with her sensual nature opens the door to burgeoning beauty or gross degradation in her own and others' lives.

Proverbs 2:16-19
Do you recognize seduction? Define elements that make a woman appear seductive.

Song of Solomon 4:1-5
If married, how would your husband describe you? Give yourself permission to be all God created you to be. How can you develop your sensual nature in a way that would please God?

Knowing and Believing
Page 183

1. Think of the last few times you have given someone advice. Describe the advice you gave.

2. Make two columns and compare earthly wisdom and wisdom from above as mentioned in James 3:13-18. How did your advice from question one measure up?

3. How does an intimate relationship with Jesus Christ help us become women who are marked by godly wisdom?

∽

Additional Study
THE INVESTIGATOR

When the female mind embraces faith in God, the potential product is staggering; conversely, her inordinate persistence of data for selfish purposes is overwhelmingly destructive.

James 1:5,26
James 3:1-10
Our investigative nature may lead us to information we wish we didn't know. How do you handle information that could hurt someone?

Judges 5:1-3
The Song of Deborah prioritizes her faith in God. Deborah was an agitator—she did excite public discussion to effect change. What can you do to present accurate information and effect change in your community?

High Yield Investment

Page 191

1. What has it cost you to be a follower of Christ?

2. What would you say to someone who wanted you to explain if it was worth the cost?

3. If you were asked to give love away to a person who is hurting and lonely, what would you do? Where would you find this person?

&

Additional Study

THE CAREGIVER

No touch to a needy person is as welcome as a caring woman; but the same touch turned against someone can be insufferably cruel.

Mark 10:13-16
Do you touch people when you talk to them? Identify appropriate ways of touching:

- a family member
- an elderly person
- a female friend
- a child
- your husband
- a male friend

Romans 8:13-14
Do you desire to become more like Jesus? Ask God to help you to be more sensitive, more sympathetic, and more loving. When a challenge to one of these qualities comes, how can you respond?

The Faith Enigma
Page 197

1. Do you really believe that God created you for honor? What is the basis for your answer?

2. What do you think is God's incredible plan for your fulfillment?

3. Read again 2 Corinthians 5:17. Write out a short prayer thanking Christ that you are a new creation because of Him.

∽

Additional Study
THE CONTROLLER

God's womanly creation has unlimited means of control but they must be tied to His principles for beneficial consequences.

Matthew 20:25-28
Identify ways you can influence people by serving rather than leading.

Scripture Index

Psalms

19	37
34:8	122
119:89	40

Proverbs

5:22	83
6:12,14	79
9:7	83
14:7,11,12	79
30:23	145
31:30	42
31:11,12	125
31:31	126

Ecclesiastes

3:11	85

Isaiah

3:16-22	193
14:12-14	48
14:13	40
40:28-31	195
40:31	95
45:6	152
46:10	40
48:17	24
52:7	85

Jeremiah

29:11-13	175

Daniel

5:27	108

Matthew

1:18-23	131
11:28-30	176
19:4	34
19:27-29	191
25:36	46

Luke

1:28-31	130
2:14	131
10:38-42	203
19-23	175

John

8	122
8:44	44
11:25	204
14:15-18	186

Acts

7:20-22	146
16:14	124
20:35	195

Romans

4:21	40
7:19	38
8:35	46
12:3	200

First Corinthians

2:6,7	185
6:19,20	161
10:11,12	201

Second Corinthians
2:14   102
5:17   202

Galatians
4:4   122

Ephesians
5:21   181
5:23   180
5:25-27   64

Philippians
4:6   174
4:13   200

Colossians
2:3   140

First Timothy
2:13,14   47
2:14   44,113

Second Timothy
1:7   200

Titus
2:4   188
21:3-5   144

Hebrews
4:16   106
5:8   198
6:18   39

Hebrews (cont.)
10:30   83
11:6   105,146
11:11   75
12:2,3   198

James
1:5   174
1:17   138
3:13-18   188
4:13-15   171

First Peter
3:1-4   179
3:1-6   75
3:3,4   42,129

Second Peter
3:9   104

Subject Index